This Book belongs To

COOKIES

SUCKER COOKIES

SUGAR COOKIES

HOLIDAY TREATS

SPOTTY

SHORT BREAD

MINT COOKIES

Christmas

Book 14

Content and Artwork by Gooseberry Patch Company

BRAVE INK PRESS

EDITORIAL STAFF
President and Editorial Director:
  Carol Field Dahlstrom
Art Director:
  Lyne Neymeyer
Photo Stylists: Carol Dahlstrom, Jennifer Peterson,
Jan Temeyer
Craft Designers: Susan Banker, Heidi Boyd,
  Susan Cage, Phyllis Dobbs, Janet Petersma,
  Ann E. Smith, Jan Temeyer
Director, Test Kitchens: Jennifer Peterson
Test Kitchens Professionals: Holly Wiederin,
  Barbara Hoover
Copy Editor: Jill Philby
Proofreader: Elizabeth Burnley
Photography: Jay Wilde Photography;
  Primary Image, Dean Tanner
Video/Communications: Dr. Michael Dahlstrom

BUSINESS STAFF
Business Manager: Judy Bailey
Webmaster: Leigha Bitz
Production Manager: Danny Epp
Props Manager: Roger H. Dahlstrom
Locations: Julie Anliker, LuAnn Brandsen
Marketing: Marcia Schultz Dahlstrom

www.braveink.com

Hardcover ISSN: 2154-4263
Softcover ISSN: 2154-4263
Hardcover ISBN-10: 0-8487-3661-3
Softcover ISBN-10: 0-8487-3659-1
Hardcover ISBN-13: 978-0-8487-3661-3
Softcover ISBN-13: 978-0-8487-3659-0
10 9 8 7 6 5 4 3 2 1

OXMOOR HOUSE
VP, Publishing Director: Jim Childs
Creative Director: Felicity Keane
Brand Manager: Vanessa Tiongson
Senior Editor: Rebecca Brennan
Managing Editor: Rebecca Benton

Gooseberry Patch Christmas Book 14
Editor: Ashley T. Strickland
Project Editor: Sarah H. Doss
Designer: Maribeth Browning
Director, Test Kitchens: Elizabeth Tyler Austin
Assistant Directors, Test Kitchens: Julie Christopher,
Julie Gunter
Test Kitchens Professionals: Wendy Ball, R.D., Allison E. Cox,
Victoria E. Cox, Margaret Monroe Dickey, Alyson Moreland
Haynes, Callie Nash, Kathleen Royal Phillips, Catherine Crowell
Steele, Leah Van Deren
Photography Director: Jim Bathie
Senior Photo Stylist: Kay E. Clarke
Associate Photo Stylist: Katherine Eckert Coyne
Assistant Photo Stylist: Mary Louise Menendez
Production Manager: Theresa Beste-Farley

CONTRIBUTORS
Photographer: Becky Luigart-Stayner
Photo Stylist: Mindi Shapiro Levine
Food Stylist: Ana Price Kelly
Interns: Laura Hoxworth, Alicia Lavender, Anna Pollock,
Ashley White

TIME HOME ENTERTAINMENT INC.
Publisher: Richard Fraiman
VP, Strategy & Business Development: Steven Sandonato
Executive Director, Marketing Services: Carol Pittard
Executive Director, Retail & Special Sales: Tom Mifsud
Director, Bookazine Development & Marketing: Laura Adam
Publishing Director: Joy Butts
Finance Director: Glenn Buonocore
Associate General Counsel: Helen Wan

Christmas

Book 14

Christmas

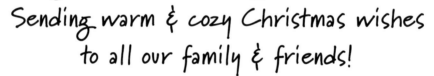

Gooseberry Patch

Sending warm & cozy Christmas wishes
to all our family & friends!

Our Story

Back in 1984, we were next-door neighbors raising our families in the little town of Delaware, Ohio. Two moms with small children, we were looking for a way to do what we loved and stay home with the kids too. We had always shared a love of home cooking and making memories with family & friends and so, after many a conversation over the backyard fence, Gooseberry Patch was born.

We put together our first catalog at our kitchen tables, enlisting the help of our loved ones wherever we could. From that very first mailing, we found an immediate connection with many of our customers and it wasn't long before we began receiving letters, photos and recipes from these new friends. In 1992, we put together our very first cookbook, compiled from hundreds of these recipes and, the rest, as they say, is history.

Hard to believe it's been over 25 years since those kitchen-table days! From that original little Gooseberry Patch family, we've grown to include an amazing group of creative folks who love cooking, decorating and creating as much as we do. Today, we're best known for our homestyle, family-friendly cookbooks, now recognized as national bestsellers.

One thing's for sure, we couldn't have done it without our friends all across the country. Each year, we're honored to turn thousands of your recipes into our collectible cookbooks. Our hope is that each book captures the stories and heart of all of you who have shared with us. Whether you've been with us since the beginning or are just discovering us, welcome to the Gooseberry Patch family!

We couldn't make our best-selling cookbooks without YOU!

Each of our books is filled with recipes from cooks just like you, gathered from kitchens all across the country.

Share your tried & true recipes with us on our website and you could be selected for an upcoming cookbook. If your recipe is included, you'll receive a FREE copy of the cookbook when it's published!

www.gooseberrypatch.com

We'd love to add YOU to our Circle of Friends!

Get free recipes, crafts, giveaways and so much more when you join our email club...join us online at all the spots below for even more goodies!

  Subscribe on **YouTube** Find us on Facebook Read Our **Blog** Follow us on **twitter**  Follow us on **Pinterest**

All Through the House

There is nothing better than coming home for Christmas! Start by filling the Christmas tree with sweet and soft ornaments surrounded by a Gingerbread House Garland to greet them. Light the way for your special guests with luminarias made from fruit jars and make them feel right at home with a Welcoming Farmhouse Basket. Add some Christmas cheer as you deck the halls with an evergreen wreath dressed in ribbons, and cozy up to a Friendly Felted Village made from recycled sweaters. Don't forget…you'll need some stockings for Santa to fill, so stitch up some Pillow Ticking Stockings in no time! It's an oh-so-wonderful Christmas in your happy holiday home!

Fabric Christmas Cookie Ornaments

Bits of rickrack, seed beads and tiny buttons combine with simple embroidery stitches to make these cookies extra-sweet.

- tracing paper
- washable marking pen
- cotton muslin fabric
- scraps of thin cotton batting
- embroidery floss in desired colors
- assorted buttons, 1/8" for gingerbread man, others as desired
- red baby rickrack for gingerbread figures
- 6 mm seed beads in assorted colors
- invisible nylon thread
- 7" of 3/8" w ribbon for each hanging loop
- scraps of felted wool, in assorted colors
- scraps of ultra-hold double-sided fusible web
- pinking shears

(continued on page 114)

Fabric Christmas Cookie Ornaments
Vintage Popcorn String

Fruit-Inspired Luminarias

Welcoming Farmhouse Basket

Create a simple basket to use as a centerpiece or as a welcome at a door. Choose a vintage egg basket or other wire basket and fill with a variety of greenery. Stuff the bottom with a green towel or tissue to cushion the eggs and to take up some of the interior space. Then fill the basket with brown eggs, fresh holly and red holly berries.

Welcoming Farmhouse Basket

Fruit-Inspired Luminarias

- clear, smooth canning jars
- tracing paper
- pencil
- scissors
- tape
- glass paint in desired colors
- paintbrush
- crackle medium, topcoat and dark crackle enhancer, such as Modern Masters
- ribbon

(continued on page 115)

Dressed-Up Wreath

A simple evergreen wreath can become a Dressed-Up Wreath for Christmas with just a little ribbon and some sliced fruit. Because the fruit dries naturally it will keep all season. A sweet Friendly Felted Village is simple and quick to stitch. It's the perfect project to showcase felted sweater fabrics and felt scraps.

Dressed-Up Wreath

- purchased evergreen wreath
- apples
- oranges
- 1 c. lemon juice
- 1 T. salt
- small bowl
- paper towels
- oven
- sharp knife
- drying rack
- 2" w plaid ribbon
- floral picks
- berry pokes

(continued on page 115)

Friendly Felted Village

The exposed seams add structure to these houses, but soft fiberfill gives them shape. Simple embroidery floss stitches attach the doors and windows. And they are child-friendly! You won't have to worry if the children knock over your display!

- assorted felted 100% wool sweaters: yellow, blue, white and beige cable. Wash sweater in hot water with detergent and tumble dry; the process should felt the wool fibers. If not, repeat the process a second time.
- 100% wool felt in white and putty colors
- 35% wool felt in pink and antique white
- polyester fiberfill
- lightweight cardboard, such as cereal boxes
- embroidery floss: light yellow, pink, beige, white, blue
- assorted buttons
- sewing machine
- scissors
- straight pins
- crewel needle

(continued on page 115)

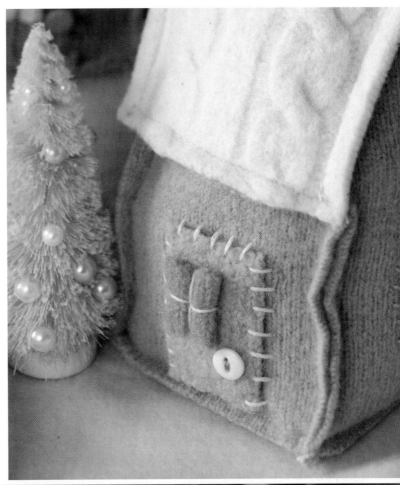

Friendly Felted Village

Pillow Ticking Stockings

Santa will love to fill these cozy stockings! Stitch up Pillow Ticking Stockings with button fringe or a soft stitched name tag. A cheery checkered Christmas tree steals the show on a Quilted Tree Table Runner and Appliquéd Tree Napkin. The table runner has nine-patch corners and a muslin quilted-tree center.

Pillow Ticking Stockings
Supplies for red stocking:
- tracing paper
- $1/2$ yard red pillow ticking fabric
- $1/3$ yard red cotton fabric
- $1/3$ yard thin fleece batting
- assorted white, off-white, tan buttons
- off-white cotton string
- off-white embroidery floss
- matching sewing thread
- tracing paper

Supplies for green stocking:
- tracing paper
- $1/2$ yard green pillow ticking fabric
- $1/3$ yard green cotton fabric
- $1/3$ yard thin fleece batting
- 2 yards 1" w lime green rickrack
- one white $5/8$" button
- matching sewing thread
- off-white embroidery floss

(continued on page 116)

Quilted Tree Table Runner
Appliquéd Tree Napkin

- tracing paper
- marking pen
- $1/2$ yard fusible webbing
- $1/2$ yard green cotton fabric
- $1/2$ yard green checked cotton fabric
- $1/4$ yard green striped fabric
- $1/4$ yard muslin fabric
- water soluble marking pen
- 20" x 32" piece thin cotton batting
- dark green embroidery or sewing thread
- light green quilting thread
- matching sewing threads

1. Trace tree patterns (page 144) onto tracing paper. Set aside. From green fabric, cut 17" square for napkin. From remaining green fabric, cut two $6^1/2$" x $18^1/2$" rectangles, twenty $2^1/2$" squares and two $6^1/2$" squares.

From muslin, cut $16^1/2$" x $18^1/2$" rectangle. From green checked fabric, cut sixteen $2^1/2$" squares and one 20" x 32" piece for backing. Trace 8 larger tree shapes onto fusible webbing and fuse to back of checked fabric. Cut out shapes.

(continued on page 116)

17

Heart♥felt Gifts They'll Love

Show how much you really care by giving the best gifts of all…gifts that are handmade by you! Delight that seamstress with a Handy Sewing Tote designed to hold all kinds of notions. A Blooming Pincushion cleverly attaches to the front pocket. Make it personal by designing a colorful painted ornament or a beaded bracelet, each complete with a unique initial. For that special person who loves to travel, create hard-working Denim Luggage Tags so those precious bags won't get lost. And don't forget the wee ones on your list…a sweet embroidered bib or crocheted hat will bring smiles to both Mommy and Baby. So have fun making gifts for everyone on your Christmas list…they'll love you for it!

Handy Sewing Tote and Blooming Pincushion
Instructions begin on page 117.

Blooming Pincushion

Handy Sewing Tote

Personalize gifts for all those special people on your list with a Reverse Painting Ornament and an Initial Bracelet. These one-of-a-kind ornaments are made using a purchased clear glass flat ornament and glass paints, painting in reverse style on the back of the piece. The charming little bracelet is strung on elastic cording. Tiny red and white print fabric makes the binding for purchased towels and creates a clever Dish Towel Apron…just in time for holiday baking. Well-worn jeans are the inspiration for Denim Luggage Tags…a perfect gift for the frequent traveler!

Reverse Painting Ornament
Initial Bracelet
instructions are on page 118.

Reverse Painting Ornament

Initial Bracelet

Dish Towel Apron

Two coordinating towels are folded and trimmed with a printed bias binding to create a favorite apron complete with big pockets.

- two 18"x28" dish towels
- ½ yard printed cotton fabric (44" w) to make tape and for waistband and belt
- 2"x 36" strip coordinated print cotton fabric for tape to edge pockets
- 1" w bias tape maker tool
- matching sewing thread

(continued on page 119)

Denim Luggage Tags

instructions are on page 118.

Dish Towel Apron

Denim Luggage Tags

This bag belongs to
NAME:
ADDRESS:
PHONE:

★ NAME:
★ ADDRESS:
★ PHONE:
★ eMaiL:

Embroidered Baby Bib

Every little one will love to wear an Embroidered Baby Bib for Christmas dinner! Sewn from tiny print fabrics, the bib has a coordinating collar and special message embroidered in the center. Dress up your little sweetheart with a Crochet Toddler Hat that sports a big happy flower.

Embroidered Baby Bib

- tracing paper
- marking pen
- fat quarter (18" x 22") cotton fabric for each bib
- 3 1/2" x 1" piece contrasting fabric for band
- scrap fabric for collar
- 11" x 15" piece thin cotton batting
- embroidery floss
- 1/2 yard of 1/4" w lace for girls' bib
- 1 1/2" long section of hook and loop tape
- three 4 3/8" buttons
- transfer paper, marking pen
- coordinating threads

1. Enlarge and trace patterns (page 145) onto tracing paper and cut out. Seams are 1/4" unless otherwise noted. Fold fat quarter of fabric in half and cut 2 bib patterns. Cut one bib pattern from batting.

2. Fold collar fabric in half to cut a total of 4 collar pieces. Cut one 3 1/2" x 12" strip from contrasting fabric for the band. Transfer lettering to center of band strip using tracing paper.

3. Using 2 or 3 strands of contrasting embroidery floss, stitch around lettering using Stem Stitch (page 139). Trim band to 2 1/2" x 10 1/2" in size. Fold 1/4" back on long edges and iron.

(continued on page 119)

Crochet Toddler Hat

Crochet abbreviations are on page 139.

Skill Level: Easy

Sizes: 1 (2, 3) years. Sizes are written for the smallest size with changes for larger sizes in parentheses. When only one number is given, it applies to all sizes.

Finished Measurements:
circumference: 16 (16 ½, 17)
length from first to last rnd:
6 (6 ¼, 6 ½)

- Caron Simply Soft, 100% acrylic yarn, (6oz/170g/315yd/288m) per skein: One skein each of Soft Green (9739) for cap and Plum Wine (9722) for flower.
- Size F/5 (3.75mm) crochet hook or size needed to obtain gauge

Gauge:
In sc, 10½ sts and 18 rows = 4"/10cm.
Take time to check your gauge.

(continued on page 119)

Crochet Toddler Hat

Crochet Toddler Hat

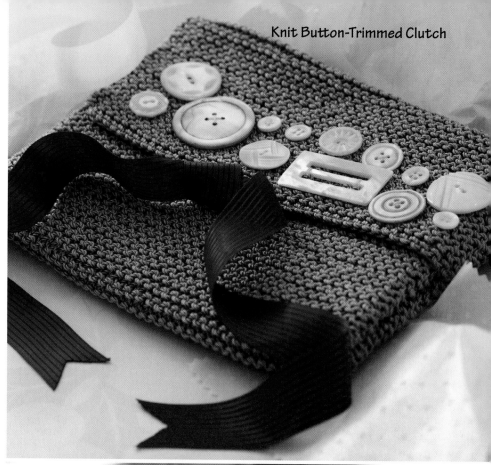

The simple garter stitch is the only stitch you use to make a Knit Button-Trimmed Clutch. Do you feel like Christmas is coming too fast? You still have time to make an Easy Fleece Hat and Scarf Set because it is a quick-sew project! Warm wool in soft colors makes a beautiful Needle Felted Sewing Case that is sure to become a treasured heirloom.

Knit Button-Trimmed Clutch

This little purse is a quick gift to make. It is simply made as a rectangle and then folded for a clutch (with some added interfacing), then finished with a variety of vintage buttons and ribbon for tying.

Skill Level: Beginner

Size: Finished bag measures approximately 8" x 6¹/₂".

- Hilos La Espiga, No.18, 100% nylon cord: One spool Delft (22)
- Size 3 (3.25 mm) knitting needles or size needed to obtain gauge
- yarn needle
- one yard of 1" w blue satin ribbon
- sewing needle and matching thread
- 7¹/₂" x 5¹/₂" piece plastic canvas
- 8" x 12" piece thin cotton batting
- 8" x 12" piece lining fabric
- assorted vintage pearl buttons

(continued on page 120)

Easy Fleece Hat and Scarf Set

Easy Fleece Hat and Scarf Set

Instructions are on page 120.

Needle Felted Sewing Case

This darling needle case is the perfect inspiration to settle down to a hand stitching project. A 100% wool felt is the ideal base for decorative needle felting while providing a thick backing for resting needles. The sweet leaf and felt bead berry ties hold the rolled felt in place.

Dimensions: 9" w x 5¾" h

- 100% wool felt in white and beige
- 35% wool felt in aqua and pale green
- off-white thread
- two $1/2$" felt beads
- wool roving in brown, beige, aqua, light blue, light green, off-white

(continued on page 121)

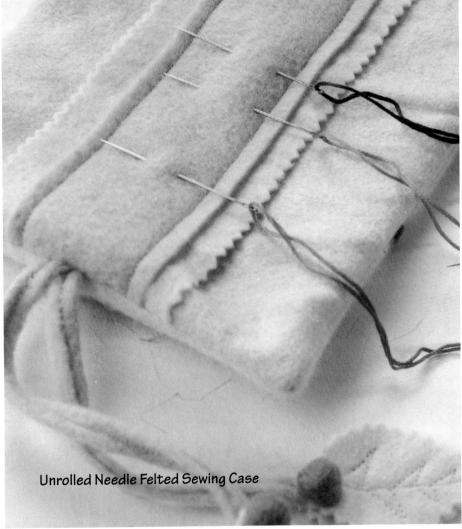

Unrolled Needle Felted Sewing Case

Country Pot Holders

- vintage 4-square quilt blocks or prepare your own from scraps of fabric (see instructions)
- 7" square of heat-resistant batting
- 7" square cotton fabric for backing
- 1⅞" x 38" cotton fabric for binding
- 20" rickrack (optional)
- 1⅛" plastic ring or 6" rickrack for hanging loop
- matching sewing thread
- perle cotton or embroidery floss if hand quilting the block

1. If making your own quilt block, cut four 3½" squares from cotton fabrics and sew together to make a 6½" block. Layer backing fabric, batting and block together.
2. Quilt block by hand or machine. Add decorative rickrack to top of block and sew through all layers

(continued on page 121)

Country Pot Holders

Don't know what to do with those favorite vintage fabric scraps? Piece 4-patch style to make them into Country Pot Holders for every cook on your Christmas list! For that special seamstress, whip up some Cupcake Pincushions that are sure to bring a smile!

Cupcake Pincushions

These clever pincushions celebrate a fascination with cupcakes. Designed using scraps of worn sweaters, the pincushions have embellishments of felt, buttons and yo-yo flowers.

For both Cupcake Pincushions:
- tracing paper
- marking pen
- small amount polyester fiberfill
- crushed walnut shells for stuffing
- matching and contrasting sewing threads

For larger Cupcake:
- 3"x 9" piece ribbing from recycled sweater (ends of sleeves or hem work great or if using a cut edge, turn a 1" hem to the back and use a walking foot to stitch in place)
- 4" square red felt
- 8" x 8" square pink cotton fabric
- 8" x 8" square lightweight iron-on interfacing
- 3" x 11" strip pink fabric
- 3" square red print fabric for yo-yo
- 3" square pink felt for bottom
- 12" piece of jumbo pink rickrack
- ³⁄₈" red button

(continued on page 121)

Christmas in the Country

During the cozy winter months, let nature provide the inspiration for holiday decorations. Making a Holiday Pomander Centerpiece or Birdie Fruit Ornaments is easy when you use the beautiful fresh fruits of the season. And all you need to do is look to the sky for the beautiful shapes of delicate snowflakes to be inspired to stitch up a Wool Snowflake Throw and matching Wool Snowflake Ornaments. Do you love the sparkle that winter brings? Capture that sparkle and share it by making Cranberry Ice Globes and displaying them at your front door for everyone to enjoy. It's a naturally beautiful time of year, so enjoy every minute of it this holiday season!

Soft Felted Nests

Nestle Soft Felted Nests in the crook of your pine boughs during the holidays or in driftwood or birch branches the rest of the year. They feature a combination of recycled and commercial felt. Die cut flowers and perky green leaves add a splash of color. Tucked into these warm little nests are a clutch of speckled polymer clay eggs. Let nature inspire you to crochet a Doe-A-Deer Stocking in rich winter colors. A contrasting checked cuff makes the stocking oh-so-festive and fun.

Soft Felted Nests
- tracing paper
- recycled sweaters in white, brown and beige
- 35% wool and 100% nonwoven felt scraps in white, off-white, wheat, vanilla and assorted green colors
- polymer clay in white, beige, aqua and light green
- oven
- off-white machine quilting thread
- assorted felted 100% wool
- sewing machine
- straight pins
- sewing needle

To felt sweaters: Wash sweater in hot water with detergent and tumble dry. The process should felt the wool fibers. If not, repeat the process a second time.

1. Enlarge and trace patterns (page 146) and cut out. Cut the nest pattern out of the felted sweater fabric. Cut the leaf shape out of a variety of green felts. Cut $1/8"$ to $1/4"$ wide by $6"$ long irregular strips of the conventional felt. These strips will become the nest branches.

2. Lay a branch strip across the nest letting it extend out either side of the nest. Machine stitch it in place. Trim the ends so they extend by $1/2"$. Snip a cut in the ends to create a forked branch. Continue adding more branches crisscrossing them over the inside and outside of the nest.

3. Bring the wedge edges together to connect and shape the nest. Machine stitch the 2 layers of

(continued on page 122)

Doe-A-Deer Stocking

Crochet abbreviations are on page 139.

Skill Level: Intermediate

Size: 16 ½" from fold of cuff to toe.

- Caron Simply Soft, 100% acrylic yarn, (6oz/170g/315yd/288m) per skein: One skein each of Garnet #0009, Bone #9703 and Forest Floor #9758
- size G/6 (4mm) crochet hook or size needed to obtain gauge
- yarn needle

Gauge: In sc, 16 sts and 16 rows = 4"/10cm.
Take time to check your gauge.

Note: To change color in sc, with present color draw up a lp then with next color complete the sc. Use separate long stands of bone when working the deer. When changing colors, carry the unused strand of yarn along top of sts and cover as you go.

Foundation:
Beginning at the top and below the cuff, with garnet, ch 49. Sc in 2nd ch from hook and in each ch across 48 sts; turn.

Row 2: Ch 1, sc in each sc across; turn.
Row 3: (begin chart, page 155): With garnet work 5 sc changing to bone in last sc for deer antlers; complete row; turn.

(continued on page 122)

Doe-A-Deer Stocking

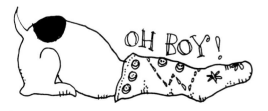

Wool Snowflake Throw

Wool Snowflake Throw

- tracing paper
- 56" x 74" piece of navy herringbone wool fabric
- matching sewing thread
- navy yarn
- 9" x 20" piece of gray wool
- 9" x 5" scrap light blue wool
- 13" x13" piece royal blue wool
- one yard lightweight fusible webbing, such as Wonder Under
- assorted colors of embroidery floss (white, light blue, dark blue) or perle cotton

1. Hem edges of wool by folding under $7/8$" along each edge and pressing. Fold again another $7/8$" to the back. Machine stitch $3/4$" from folded edge along all edges, pivoting at corners. Using navy yarn, sew large blanket or buttonhole stitches around all outside edges of the throw, using sewing line as a guide for depth of stitches.

2. Enlarge and trace a total of 12 snowflake patterns (page 147). Trace onto the paper of fusible webbing. Iron the webbing to the back of wool pieces. Cut out shapes. Fuse 3 different snowflake shapes for each corner of the wool throw. Use a combination of hand and machine stitches to sew around outside edges of snowflakes. Use 3 strands of embroidery floss or single thread of perle cotton to embroider decorative stitches onto snowflake shapes.

3. Embroidery stitches used: Blanket Stitch, Stem Stitch, Running Stitch, French Knot, Chain Stitch, Backstitch, Straight Stitch, Fern Stitch and Fly Stitch. See pages 137–139 for diagrams.

Cuddle up and keep toasty warm in a Wool Snowflake Throw. This cozy throw is appliquéd with snowflake shapes inspired by the beautiful snowflakes that winter brings! Create your own Wool Snowflake Ornaments from felted wool and simple embroidery stitches. Remember…no two are alike!

Wool Snowflake Ornaments

Wool Snowflake Ornaments

- tracing paper
- two 6" squares of felted wool in blue, gray or white colors
- assorted felt scraps in blue, gray or white colors
- heavyweight fusible webbing
- embroidery floss or perle cotton in white, light blue and dark blue colors
- 8" length fine silver cord or perle cotton for hanging loop
- matching sewing threads
- tracing paper

1. Trace patterns (page 147) onto tracing paper and cut out. Trace desired pattern onto fusible webbing paper, fuse to the back of wool fabrics and cut out.
2. Fold length of hanging loop in half and insert ends between two layers of larger shapes.
3. Layer shapes as desired and fuse in place.
4. Machine or hand stitch around outside edges of ornaments and embellish with coordinating threads of either 2 strands embroidery floss or perle cotton. Stitches used include Blanket Stitch, Stem Stitch, French Knot, Fern Stitch, Lazy Daisy Stitch, Backstitch and Chain Stitch. See pages 137–139 for diagrams.

Holiday Pomander Centerpiece

Cranberry Ice Globes

Holiday Pomander Centerpiece

Citrus fruits are studded with whole cloves and other spices to make a naturally aromatic centerpiece.

- fresh oranges, lemons and limes
- pencil
- round toothpick
- whole cloves
- woven basket
- fresh evergreens
- acorns and pine cones (optional)

1. Wash and dry the fruit to be used.

2. Choose the desired piece of fruit. With a pencil, mark dots where you want to place the whole cloves. Make patterns such as little stars, lines to form rows or snowflake patterns.

3. Use the toothpick to make a hole at each dot. Press the whole clove into the hole pushing in securely. Repeat for the other fruits to be used.

4. Arrange the fruits in the woven basket. Add fresh greens, acorns, pinecones, cinnamon sticks or other natural embellishments as desired. This centerpiece will stay fresh for approximately 4 days if kept in a cool place.

Cranberry Ice Globes

Instructions are on page 123.

Making a Holiday Pomander Centerpiece is so easy and brings a sweet aroma to your holiday home. Cranberry Ice Globes are almost magical! The water and cranberries are frozen together inside a round balloon to form the shape. With fresh fruit, peanut butter and birdseed, you can make Birdie Fruit Ornaments. Your feathered friends will love you!

Birdie Fruit Ornaments: Birdie Apple Treat, Birdie Orange and Kiwi Cups

- apples
- awl
- table knife
- small star cookie cutter
- peanut butter
- orange
- kiwi
- sharp knife; spoon
- fine twine
- birdseed

1. **For the Birdie Apple Treat,** slice the apple in 1/4" slices. Using the cookie cutter, cut the shape from the middle of the apple. Spread peanut butter on the star cutout and the apple slice. Sprinkle with birdseed. Poke a hole at the top of the apple slice using the awl. Thread the twine through the hole to hang on the tree.

2. **For the Orange Cup and Kiwi Cup,** slice the fruit in half and scoop out fruit. Use the awl to poke a hole in each side of cup and tie the twine in the holes. Fill with birdseed and hang on the tree.

Birdie Apple Treat

Birdie Orange Cup

Birdie Kiwi Cup

There will be smiles on Christmas morning when the little ones see what Santa has brought them this year! Simple cardstock is cut into paper doll dress shapes and covered with bits of fabric and embellishments to make Paper Doll Dress Trims for the holiday tree. Little gingerbread cookies are tucked into folded bandannas and favorite candies become sparkling little ornaments. Sweet Sister Dolls are stitched from socks, making them soft, lovable and no doubt a favorite toy. Be sure to use children's art and wrap those special packages to make this the perfect holiday for every boy and girl.

Sweet Sister Dolls

Salt Clay Snowflakes

A simple salt clay recipe yields dozens of snowflakes that are easily decorated with permanent markers. Cookie cutters make cutting the shapes oh-so-easy.

- one recipe Cornstarch Clay
- snowflake cookie cutter
- rolling pin
- drinking straw
- drying rack or foil
- fine-tip permanent marker in desired color
- narrow ribbon

1. Mix up Cornstarch Clay recipe (page 123) and keep in plastic bags until ready to use.
2. Roll out the clay onto a smooth surface, rolling to about ¼" thick. Cut out clay shapes using a snowflake cookie cutter or other desired cookie cutter.
3. Use a drinking straw to make the hole at the top of the ornament shape for hanging.
4. Arrange the cut pieces on a drying rack or foil and allow to dry for about 3 hours or overnight. Turn shapes over halfway through the drying time.

(continued on page 123)

Sweet Sister Dolls
Child's Art Wraps
Instructions are on pages 123 and 124.

Child's Art Wraps

Salt Clay Snowflakes

Paper Doll Dress Trims

The cute and cuddly Sweet Sister Dolls are sewn in the style of old-fashioned sock dolls. Roll out a simple clay recipe to make Salt Clay Snowflakes. Nothing is more original than using favorite artwork for Child's Art Wraps. Children become fashion designers when they make Paper Doll Dress Trims.

Paper Doll Dress Trims

- various fabric scraps
- cardstock or poster board
- crafts glue
- scissors
- tracing or transfer paper
- small buttons, ribbon and rickrack to match fabric
- black permanent marker
- thin fusible interfacing
- iron
- dark lead pencil
- flat paint brush (optional)
- thread for buttons

1. Enlarge and trace clothing patterns (page 150) onto poster board using transfer paper or using a copier on card stock; cut out. Using the pencil, trace patterns onto right sides of fabric excluding the tabs.

2. Before cutting out fabric, iron a small square of fusible interfacing onto wrong side of fabric, where the outfit is traced following manufacturer's instructions.

Note: There is no need to add interfacing to collars, cuffs, sailor skirt, mittens or front dress facing.

3. When the fabric is cooled, cut out all clothing and add any small decorative pieces.

(continued on page 124)

Fold up a hankie, add a touch of paint and you've made a Bandanna Art Trim…perfect for sharing holiday treats. Sweet Candy Ornaments are made by melting colorful hard candy into fun, kid-friendly shapes. Little fingers will love to wear Santa Family Finger Puppets to tell all about their Christmas adventures with Santa Claus.

Bandanna Art Trim

- purchased bandanna in desired colors
- scissors
- fabric paint pens
- embroidery floss to match bandanna color
- needle
- parchment paper
- cookies or treats to fill trim

(continued on page 124)

Sweet Candy Ornament
Instructions are on page 125.

Bandanna Art Trim

Sweet Candy Ornament

Child's Art Wrap

Elf Puppets

Santa Family Finger Puppets

Santa Family Finger Puppets

- tracing paper
- cardstock
- colored pencils or crayons
- scissors
- small scraps of felt
- crafts glue
- pom-poms for hats
- tiny button for collar

1. Trace the patterns (page 149). Copy onto cardstock and cut out. Cut out a set of 2 patterns for the Santa Puppets.

2. For the Elf Puppets, use colored pencils to color in the areas as desired. Cut out. Cut a slit where marked on the tab. Bend and fasten tab and slide on fingers.

3. For the Mr. and Mrs. Claus Puppets, color faces with colored pencils. Cut hat, beard and collar pieces from additional pattern. Draw around the pieces onto felt. Glue felt to colored pieces. Glue pom-poms and button in place. Cut a slit where marked on the tab. Bend and fasten tab and slide on fingers.

STITCH iT UP for CHRISTMAS

Whether you like to sew, crochet, quilt or embroider, you'll love using your stitching talents to make the season bright! Christmas-red yarn magically turns into a Crochet Poinsettia Blossom to decorate the tree or a special package. Printed holiday motifs on old-fashioned hankies provide the color and pattern for Vintage Handkerchief Pillows to toss in a favorite chair. Soft felt in bright holiday colors makes Cozy Mug Wraps for everyone who comes to share a cup of cocoa. You'll have fun choosing a combination of tiny prints to make Mother/Daughter Country Aprons with prairie point edges or an easy-to-make lamp shade. So settle into your cozy chair and start stitching up some Christmas joy to share.

Vintage Handkerchief Pillows

These little pillows can be filled with sachet or just tossed in groups for a festive look.

- one or two vintage Christmas hankies for each pillow
- cotton fabrics for front and/or back of pillows
- matching sewing thread
- polyester fiberfill
- purchased piping or cording and fabric for piping
- buttons, beads, ribbon trims and other embellishments

1. Look at handkerchiefs to see what parts can be used and experiment with layouts and combinations of coordinating fabrics before starting.
Note: Some handkerchiefs have perfect borders for gathering for a ruffle around a smaller pillow. Others may have worn spots or stains but a center design is good. The pillows shown are 8"-9" in size.
2. After deciding the design of the pillow and pieces needed, hand sew parts of hankies onto coordinating cotton fabrics or iron fusible webbing onto the back of designs to cut out and fuse to another piece of handkerchief or coordinating fabric.
3. Add small bits of ribbon, old buttons, tiny beads or yo-yo's (a 5$\frac{1}{2}$" circle makes a finished 2$\frac{1}{4}$" yo-yo) for decoration to pillow front.
4. Make piping by covering cording or purchase piping to sew around the outside edge of the pillow or use as a decorative inset trim.
5. With right sides together, stitch the pillow front to the pillow back using $\frac{1}{4}$" seams, leaving an opening for turning.
6. Trim across corners and turn. Stuff pillow. Slip stitch opening closed using matching sewing thread.

Vintage Handkerchief Pillows

Easy Holiday Lamp Shade

- ½ yard green and white stripe fabric
- coordinating sewing thread
- scissors
- one spool (about 30 inches) red pom-pom fringe

1. Measure the lamp shade around the bottom edge and add 5" to the width for length measurement. Measure the height of the lamp shade and add 2½" to the height for height measurement. Cut one piece using the measurements width x height.

2. Use ¼" seam allowance, unless otherwise instructed, and sew with right sides together. Press seams as you sew.

3. Sew the side edges together (the short ends).

4. Fold a double ¼" hem on the top edge and sew.

5. Fold a ¼" hem, then a 1" hem on the bottom edge and sew.

6. Sew a gathering stitch ¾" from the top edge. Start pulling gathers. Place the cover on top of the lamp shade and pull gathers to hold in place so that the lamp shade top and bottom edges do not show. Tie gathering thread. Space gathers evenly and topstitch on top of the gathers to hold in place.

7. Pin the pom-pom fringe on the bottom edge and hand or machine sew to the lamp cover. Repeat, sewing the pom-pom fringe at top of shade, covering the gathers.

Easy Holiday Lamp Shade

Motifs from pretty Christmas hankies are stitched and appliquéd to create Vintage Handkerchief Pillows. Add tiny beads to the center of the blooms for some Christmas sparkle. Make reading those favorite holiday stories even more special by creating an Easy Holiday Lamp Shade. A pretty pom-pom edging adds the finishing touch to this simple little accessory.

**Monogram
Wool Stocking**

Monogram Wool Stocking

Vintage buttons embellish the toe and heel of this traditional wool pattern stocking.

- tracing paper
- marking pen
- $^1/_2$ yard red wool fabric
- $^1/_3$ yard plaid flannel fabric
- $^1/_8$ yard gray wool fabric
- 1$^3/_4$ yard of $^1/_4$" cording
- $^1/_3$ yard of fusible interfacing
- assorted vintage buttons
- $^1/_8$" decorative red cording for monogram letters
- matching sewing threads
- light-colored carbon paper

1. Enlarge and trace patterns (page 151) onto tracing paper and cut out. From red wool fabric, cut 1$^1/_2$" strips of 45" and 16" lengths to cover cording, cut 2 from stocking pattern for lining, one each from heel and toe patterns and one 2"x 9" strip for hanging loop. From plaid fabric, cut 2 from stocking pattern. From gray fabric, cut 4 from cuff pattern. From interfacing, cut 2 from stocking pattern.

(continued on page 125)

Cozy Mug Wraps

Crochet Poinsettia Blossom

Warm, woolly and waiting to be filled with holiday goodies, our Monogram Wool Stocking is personalized with red cording. Shadow quilting is the technique used to make Cozy Mug Wraps…such a pretty way to dress up winter mugs for holiday entertaining. Don't you just love the bright color of Christmas poinsettias? Create your own holiday blooms by making a Crochet Poinsettia Blossom using bright red yarn.

Cozy Mug Wraps

- tracing paper
- marking pen
- scissors/pinking shears (optional)
- felt scraps, assorted colors
- matching sewing thread
- 14" of ¼"w ribbon for each wrap

1. Enlarge and trace inside and outside wrap patterns (page 152) onto tracing paper and cut out. Trace full-size Christmas motifs (page 152) onto tracing paper and cut figures apart. Cut one each of wrap inside and outside strips from coordinating colors felt. Pinking shears may be used to add interest to cut edges. Cut length of ribbon in half to make two 7" lengths.
2. Center inside strip over outside strip and pin in place. Center ribbon and insert between layers at ends.
3. Stitch close to cut edges of inside strip, stitching through both layers of felt, backstitching over ribbon ends. Center motif pattern on back side of wrap and pin in place.
4. Using thread to match front inside strip felt color, stitch around lines of motif from the back side of the wrap. On front side cut away front layer of felt where desired to expose back felt layer below. Cut close to stitching lines and remove sections of front layer of felt.
5. Place the finished wrap around tumbler or cup and tie in place. Wrap can be used to insulate beverage container or as an identifier for each person's container.

Crochet Poinsettia Blossom
Instructions are on page 125.

Stitch up a Bias Tape Birdie Set to use during special holiday get-togethers. The Striped Pot Holder has an outside pocket and simple French-knot details. The Birdie Tea Towel sports pretty winter birds and the Plaid-Trimmed Table Runner is trimmed in overlapped bias tape forming a simple plaid design.

Striped Pot Holder
Plaid-Trimmed Table Runner

Bias Tape Birdie Set

Inspired by a 1920s tea towel, this stitched kitchen set uses colorful bias tape and simple embroidery stitches.

Plaid-Trimmed Table Runner

- one white tea towel (approximately 18" x 27")
- 2 5/8 yards red extra wide double fold bias tape
- 2 5/8 yards **each** blue and green single fold bias tape
- matching threads
- gold embroidery floss

1. Stitch bias tapes to towel, starting with green tape placed 1/2" from outside edge of long side of towel. Pin in place, folding cut edge under 1/2" to back of towel.
2. Stitch close to both side edges using matching thread. Repeat process on short ends of towel, crossing tape at corners.

3. Place blue tape 1/4" from edge of green tape and stitch in place. Place wide red tape 1/4" from edge of blue tape and stitch in place.
4. Using 3 strands embroidery floss, make French knots between bias tape rows.

Birdie Tea Towel

- one white dish towel (approximately 18"x 27")
- four 5" strips of single fold bias tape for birds
- 2 1/2" and 6 1/2" lengths green single fold bias tape for branch
- black embroidery floss
- gold embroidery floss
- matching sewing threads

1. Referring to pattern (page 153), place green bias tape approximately 3 1/2" from bottom edge of towel. Place smaller branch on towel first and pin in place. Hand stitch in place using matching sewing thread. Sew with small stitches through toweling and tape. Fold cut edge under at top edge.
2. Place longer piece of green tape over lower cut edge of short branch. Pin in place and stitch with small hand stitches. Make birds by placing bottom piece of tape in place first, folding under edges

(continued on page 126)

Bias Tape Birdie Tea Towel

One of the best parts of Christmas is baking together as a family! Choose vintage-style prints to make treasured Mother/Daughter Country Aprons. Pieced in 9-patch or 4-patch style, Patchwork Calico Pillows are quick to make in happy holiday colors.

Mother/Daughter Country Aprons

Mother/Daughter Country Aprons

Mother's apron:
- ¹/₂ yard yellow print fabric
- ¹/₂ yard red print fabric
- ¹/₈ yard green print fabric
- ¹/₈ yard stripe fabric
- coordinating sewing thread

Daughter's apron:
- ¹/₄ yard yellow print fabric
- ¹/₄ yard red print fabric
- ¹/₈ yard green print fabric
- ¹/₈ yard stripe fabric
- coordinating sewing thread

Mother's apron:
From yellow fabric, cut one piece 36¹/₂" x 4¹/₂".
From red fabric, cut waist band 4¹/₄" x 64" (piece to get this length).

(continued on page 126)

Mother Country Apron

Patchwork Calico Pillows

For green pillow:
- cotton fabric scraps to make thirty-six 2¹/₂" squares

For red pillow:
- cotton fabric for four 6¹/₂" squares
- two 1³/₄" buttons
- upholstery thread

For both pillows:
- fabric to cover cording
- thread to match fabrics
- 1³/₈ yard piping-style cording
- 12¹/₂" square piece of batting
- 12¹/₂" square piece of muslin
- 12¹/₂" square cotton fabric for backing
- 12" pillow form or polyester fiberfill to stuff pillow cover

1. For green pillow: Sew 36 squares together in strips of 6 squares each, then combine the strips to complete a 12¹/₂" square pillow top using ¹/₄" seams.
For red pillow: Sew 4 squares together to complete a 12¹/₂" square pillow top.
For both pillows: Layer top, batting and muslin pieces and baste together. Quilt as desired.
2. Cut fabric into 1¹/₂" strips to cover cording. Join together to make approximately 54" long strip. Wrap fabric around cording, wrong sides together. Sew closely to cording, using a zipper foot. Sew cording to pillow top, keeping raw edges of cording even with raw edges of top.

(continued on page 127)

Daughter
Country Apron

Patchwork Calico Pillows

Handmade Greetings and Gift Wraps

Making the outside of the gift as pretty as the inside is half the fun of giving! So gather together some unexpected supplies and make one-of-a-kind Package Toppers and clever gift wraps. Making your own Christmas cards and tags shows that you really care! Bits of fabric, holiday stickers and scrapbook papers will inspire you. Your friends & family will be delighted with the heartfelt greetings you share.

Buttons and Bows Topper instructions are on page 128.

Patterned cupcake liners, jingle bells, buttons, toys, sheet music and paper poinsettias are the center of attention when they become Pretty Package Toppers for your holiday gifts.

Cupcake Liner Topper and Box

Choose your favorite cupcake liners for inside and out of the box. Stack them for a ruffled bow on the lid, then use them inside as compartments to hold a few of her favorite things!

- shallow box to fit 4-6 cupcake liners
- cupcake liners in coordinating patterns
- cardstock/patterned paper in colors to match cupcake liners
- ribbon
- stapler
- circle punches in 3 sizes
- adhesive–including tape, foam dots and stapler

Inside of box:

1. Make dividers for box by cutting 2 strips of cardstock the same depth as the box base–one for the width and one for the length of the box.
2. Cut a slit in the center of each strip and interlock them.
3. Invert the cupcake liners and place in sections of box.

(continued on page 127)

Toy Topper
Jingle Bell Topper
Instructions are on page 127.

Jingle Bell Topper/
Cupcake Liner Topper

To:
From:

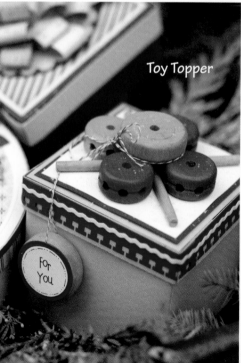

Toy Topper

For You

Cupcake Liner Box

Pretty Package Toppers

Buttons and Bows Topper

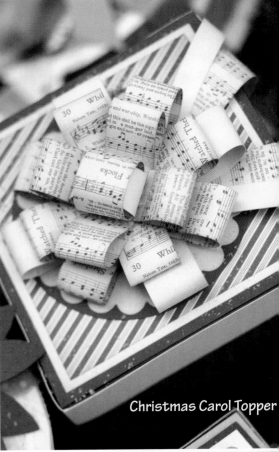

Christmas Carol Topper

How stripes get on the peppermints

Poinsettia Topper

- tracing paper
- cardboard box
- 3 colors coordinating cardstock
- 2 patterned papers
- green striped/dot paper for leaves
- circle punches for flower centers
- pearl gems
- foam dots
- tape adhesive

1. Cover box and lid with cardstock using strong tape adhesive. Trim with a narrow strip of cardstock. Cover edge of lid with patterned paper. Layer top of lid with mats of coordinating cardstock/paper.

2. Trace pattern (page 154) onto tracing paper. Cut poinsettias from cardstock and leaves from green striped/dot paper. Adhere the flowers and leaves to lid using foam dots. Punch circles for the center of each flower. Adhere pearl gems to the center of the largest flower.

Paper Poinsettia Topper

Buttons and Bows Topper
Christmas Carol Topper
Instructions are on page 128.

Tiny felt sweaters keep pets warm when they become Dressed-Up Doggy Cards. Do you have fabric scraps too pretty to toss? Use those favorite prints to silhouette Christmas motifs for Fabric-Backed Cards. Tear it, stamp it or embellish it…you've created a trio of Wraps in Brown Paper.

Dressed-Up Doggy Cards
- 8¹/2" x 11" sheet of natural cardstock or white cardstock (each sheet will make 2 cards)
- tan, white and brown solid card stock paper scraps
- patterned aqua and off-white dotted scrapbook paper
- small scraps of red and aqua wool felt
- aqua chalk stamp pad
- black stamp pad
- message rubber stamp
- snowflake rubber stamp
- embroidery floss in red and off-white
- crewel needle
- crafts glue and glue stick
- fine point permanent marker
- scissors

Lady and Fido will love to see themselves on your Christmas cards this year!

(continued on page 128)

Fabric-Backed Cards
Instructions begin on page 128.

Poodle Doggy Card

Dachshund Doggy Card

Fabric-Backed Cards

Stamped Paper Bag

Wraps in Brown Paper

HOLLY JOLLY GREETINGS!
TO:
FROM:

HAPPY HOLIDAYS
TO:
FROM:

Woodland Wrap

- paper maché box
- cardstock in 3 shades of green plus white, brown
- snowflakes—felt, punched, die cut or stickers
- small pine cone
- strong tape adhesive
- foam dots
- stapler
- hot-glue gun and glue sticks
- embossing template
- circle punch

(continued on page 129)

Stamped Paper Bag
Torn Paper Wrap

Instructions are on page 129.

Woodland Wrap

Torn Paper Wrap

HAPPY HOLIDAYS
TO:
FROM:

Purchased stickers or die cuts convey sweet holiday messages on Warm Wishes and There's No Place Like Home Cards. Gift-Giving Purses hide little gift cards inside while remaining stylish on the outside. Merry Gift Tags are the perfect way to say, "To you from me!"

Warm Wishes Snowman Card

- large rectangular snowman image (sticker, die cut, stamp or clip art)
- 3 colors of cardstock to match
- 2 coordinated patterned papers
- tab die or punch
- tulle
- narrow ribbon
- button
- punched snowflake
- self-adhesive jewels
- embossing template
- adhesive—including adhesive dimensional dots
- ink for edging paper
- computer or stamps for inside greeting

1. Cut card base from cardstock. Score and fold so that card opens at right side.
2. Emboss pattern in the top portion of the card front.
3. Ink edges of card; lightly ink embossed pattern.
4. Cut strip of patterned paper; ink and adhere across lower portion of card. Cut wider strip of cardstock and adhere just above patterned paper.

(continued on page 130)

There's No Place Like Home Card
Instructions are on page 130.

Warm Wishes Snowman Card

There's No Place Like Home Card

Gift-Giving Purses

Pink Patterned Purse Card

- scalloped purse and topper patterns
- heavy double-sided patterned paper
- 2 colors coordinating cardstock
- small hole punch
- button
- floss
- cording for handle
- coordinated ribbon
- adhesive—including fine-tipped adhesive and glue dots
- computer or stamps for inside greeting

(continued on page 130)

Holly Purse Card
Tinsel Purse Card
Merry Gift Tags

Instructions are on pages 130 and 131.

Merry Gift Tags

In A Twinkling

Sit back and enjoy this wonderful season…you still have time to make plenty of projects just in time for Christmas! In the blink of an eye you can make a pretty wreath with simple supplies you find at the crafts store or in your kitchen. No time to sew those fancy tree trims? Just use a little glue to make No-Sew Fabric Trims. Use purchased cut-out letters to spread the joy all around your house…just add your own special touches with a little paint and some buttons. So relax and enjoy the season…you've made those last-minute handmade projects just in the nick of time.

"Joy" Decoration instructions are on page 132.

"Joy" Decoration

Reindeer Wreath

Want a simple but clever wreath to decorate your door this year? Take a trip to the crafts store and be inspired by the ribbons and supplies available. A Reindeer Wreath sports a reindeer-motif design on the ribbon. Or look in your kitchen drawer to make a Cookie Cutter Wreath by wiring your favorite cutters on the wreath. Have fun wrapping foam balls with white yarn to create little snowmen. Then dress them up for winter to decorate your Happy Snowmen Wreath.

Reindeer Wreath
- fresh green wreath
- vintage or new small reindeer
- red jingle bells
- ribbon with reindeer motif
- 24-gauge wire

1. Wrap wreath with ribbon securing in the back. Add a ribbon tie at the bottom.
2. Wire jingle bells to the wreath between ribbon.
3. Secure reindeer in the center of the wreath. Add wire for hanging.

Cookie Cutter Wreath
- fresh green wreath
- vintage or new cookie cutters in desired shapes
- 2" w checked fabric ribbon
- 3" w ribbon for bow
- 24-gauge wire
- small vintage rolling pins

Cookie Cutter Wreath

Happy Snowmen Wreath

1. Lay wreath on covered surface. Wind checked ribbon around the wreath.

2. Wire cookie cutters and rolling pin onto the wreath. Make a large bow and wire to the top of wreath.

Happy Snowmen Wreath

- 3" foam balls, such as Styrofoam
- lightweight white cotton batting scraps
- crafts glue
- white cotton yarn
- tracing paper
- pencil
- orange felt scraps for noses
- black glass round 8 mm beads for eyes
- black glass 3 x 4 mm donut beads for mouth
- scraps of felt, fleece or felted wool for hats, scarves
- scraps from discarded knit sweater for ear muffs and long pointed hat
- coordinating colors embroidery floss
- 2 cotton balls for ear muffs
- matching sewing thread

(continued on page 132)

Country Apple Candles

Snowflakes Under Glass

Country Apple Candles

A muffin tin becomes a country candle holder when you add red and green apples that have been carved out to hold votive candles. The apple candle holders rest in each muffin cup.

• muffin tin
• sharp knife
• apples (red or green)
• small votive candles

1. Place the votive candle on top of the apple and mark where to cut for the opening. Use the knife to cut a hole slightly larger than the candle.
2. Place the candle into the hole made in the apple. Place the apples in the muffin tin.

Snowflakes Under Glass
Instructions begin on page 132.

No-Sew Fabric Trims

No-Sew Fabric Trims

These fabric ornaments look highly embellished but they are actually a no-sew project. The edges of the fabric scraps are pushed into the foam balls and the seams covered with rickrack.

- tracing paper
- scissors
- pencil
- 3" foam ball, such as Styrofoam
- sharp knife
- scraps of small print fabric
- crafts glue
- scraps of small trims, such as rickrack

(continued on page 133)

Use the beautiful colors of red and green apples to carve out Country Apple Candles for a quick centerpiece. Let the children help cut pretty snowflakes to make Snowflakes Under Glass that everyone will love. Just a little glue and a few scraps of print fabric make special No-Sew Fabric Trims. Twine-Tied Candles come together in minutes and add sparkle to your holiday event.

Twine-Tied Candles

Twine-Tied Candles
Instructions are on page 133.

Gifts from the Country Kitchen

Share your sweet cooking talents with those you love by making gifts from your kitchen! How about mixing up some Orange-Macadamia Fudge and then tucking the pieces in a decorated tin? You'll be helping a busy friend with their last-minute party when you present a jar of Pretzels with Pizzazz…they're ready to serve! Grandma's Zucchini Bread will be a family favorite (so be sure to make plenty for yourself as well). With 15 yummy recipes and clever wrap ideas, you'll have a great time stirring up the perfect gift for everyone on your Christmas list.

Cheddar Cheese Crispies
Cracker Tin

Cheddar Cheese Crispies

A quick & easy snack! For a spicier flavor, add a little more cayenne pepper, a little black pepper and a dash of dry mustard.

8-oz. pkg. shredded sharp Cheddar cheese
1 c. butter, softened
2 c. all-purpose flour
$1/2$ t. salt
$1/4$ t. cayenne pepper
2 c. crispy rice cereal

Combine cheese and butter; mix well. Let stand for a few minutes to soften. Add remaining ingredients; mix well. Shape into about 2 dozen balls and flatten slightly to about $1/4$ to $1/2$-inch thick. Place on ungreased baking sheets. Bake at 350 degrees for 15 to 20 minutes, until lightly browned around the edges. Makes about 2 dozen.

Lorrie Smith
Drummonds, TN

Cracker Tin

- metal can with lid
- small pieces of white/solid/patterned cardstock
- adhesive dimensional dots
- stamps, rub-on letters or computer/printer
- $3/4$" hole punch (to fit magnets)
- small snowflake punch
- $3/4$" magnets
- glitter glue

1. For Tag: Print text onto white cardstock, allowing room for tree at left. Print or stamp border around text. From cardstock or patterned paper, cut a triangle tree and trunk. Adhere to tag using adhesive dimensional dots.
2. For Magnets: Punch $3/4$" circles from cardstock or patterned paper and adhere to magnet fronts. Punch small snowflakes to fit magnets and adhere. Add a dot of glitter glue to each snowflake and allow to dry.
3. Secure tag to can with magnets. Add other magnets to the can if desired.

Peggy's Granola
Tent Card

Package Peggy's Granola, so crunchy and honey-sweet, in individual bags and add a patterned tent-style tag to announce the gift. Everyone will be eager to read their fortune so cleverly tucked inside Jumbo Fortune Cookies. Present the sweet treats in a take-out box you make yourself.

Peggy's Granola

When a dear friend put this granola in a gift basket, my husband and I couldn't stop eating it!

4 c. quick-cooking oats, uncooked
2 c. crispy rice cereal
2 c. sliced almonds
2 T. cinnamon
2 c. brown sugar, packed
$^2/_3$ c. butter
$^1/_2$ c. honey
2 c. chopped dried fruit or raisins

Toss oats, cereal, almonds and cinnamon together in a large bowl; set aside. Combine brown sugar, butter and honey in a heavy saucepan over medium-high heat. Boil, stirring occasionally, until butter is melted and brown sugar is dissolved. Pour over oat mixture; stir to coat. Spread evenly on an aluminum foil-lined baking sheet. Bake at 350 degrees for 10 minutes; stir well. Bake for an additional 10 minutes. Remove from oven and cool 5 minutes; transfer to a large bowl. Stir in raisins or fruit and cool completely. Store in airtight containers. Makes 14 cups.

*Beth Smith
Manchester, MI*

Tent Card instructions are on page 133.

a sweet treat

Jumbo Fortune Cookies

Good fortune is sure to smile on you when you give these cookies!

4 egg whites
1 c. superfine sugar
1 c. all-purpose flour, sifted
$^1/_8$ t. salt
$^1/_4$ c. plus 1 T. butter, melted
3 T. whipping cream
1 t. almond extract
melted white chocolate
red, green and white sugars

Write fortunes on strips of paper about 4" long and $^1/_2$" wide. Beat together egg whites and sugar; add flour and salt, mixing well. Blend in remaining ingredients except melted chocolate and colored sugars. Pour one tablespoon batter onto half of a baking sheet coated with non-stick vegetable spray; spread with a spoon into a 5-inch circle. Repeat on other half. Bake at 400 degrees for 8 minutes, or until edges turn golden. Working quickly, slice a spatula under cookies; lift and place on a dish towel. Place a fortune on each cookie, close to the middle. Fold cookies in half, pinching at top to form a loose semicircle. Place the folded edge across the rim of a measuring cup and pull the pointed edges down, one on the inside of the cup and one on the outside; allow to harden. Repeat with remaining batter. Dip edges in melted chocolate; immediately dip in colored sugar. Makes 18.

Fortune Cookie Box instructions are on page 134.

**Jumbo Fortune Cookies
Fortune Cookie Box**

For You

Pack spicy Apple-Ginger Chutney into little canning jars...then add a colorful paper topper for a perfect presentation. Stir up a batch of Grandma's Zucchini Bread in no time. A little vintage-looking paper apron becomes a keepsake tag.

Apple-Ginger Chutney

When we had Sunday dinner at my grandparents' house, Gran always had extra jars of this fruity, spicy relish for us to take home. It's delicious on roasted or grilled chicken...try it spooned over cream cheese on a cracker too. Yum!

4 Granny Smith apples, cored, peeled and chopped
2 c. onion, minced
1 red pepper, minced
1/4 c. fresh ginger, peeled and minced
1 c. golden raisins
1 1/2 c. cider vinegar
1 1/2 c. dark brown sugar, packed
3/4 t. dry mustard
3/4 t. salt
1/2 t. red pepper flakes
6 1/2-pint canning jars and lids, sterilized

Combine all ingredients in a large saucepan over medium-high heat. Bring to a boil, stirring frequently. Reduce heat to low. Simmer for 40 minutes, stirring occasionally, until thickened. Spoon chutney into sterilized jars; cool slightly and add lids. Keep refrigerated up to 2 weeks. Makes 6 jars.

Anna McMaster
Portland, OR

Jar Topper instructions are on page 134.

Apple-Ginger Chutney
Jar Topper

Grandma's Zucchini Bread

Growing up, my favorite harvest memory was getting the chance to go over to my grandma's house. She would let me go out into the yard and pick the zucchini. We'd then use the best ones to make this bread. She would let me set out the ingredients and do the mixing, and afterward, we'd talk and enjoy slices of her delicious zucchini bread.

3 c. all-purpose flour
1 t. salt
$^1/_4$ t. baking powder
1 t. baking soda
1 T. cinnamon
3 eggs
1 c. oil
2 t. vanilla extract
$2^1/_4$ c. sugar
2 zucchini, shredded
$^1/_2$ c. chopped walnuts

Sift flour, salt, baking powder, baking soda and cinnamon together; set aside. Beat eggs, oil, vanilla and sugar together; add to flour mixture and blend well. Stir in zucchini and nuts until well combined. Pour batter into 2 lightly greased 8"x 4" loaf pans. Bake at 325 degrees for 55 to 65 minutes. Cool in pans on a wire rack for 20 minutes. Remove from pans and cool. Makes 2 loaves.

Stefanie Schmidt
Las Vegas, NV

Apron Tag

- tracing paper
- 2-3 coordinated patterned papers and cardstock
- ribbon
- border punch
- small circle punch
- light tan ink
- embossing template or folder
- stamps, rub-on letters or computer/printer

1. Enlarge and trace pattern (page 155). Cut dress body from patterned paper. Emboss the skirt and lightly ink.
2. Cut small rectangle from coordinating patterned paper and adhere to the center of the dress top. Adhere a strip of narrow ribbon to either side of the dress, leaving length to tie.
3. Print or stamp "Grandma's Zucchini Bread" (or other name) on white cardstock. Cut out and then use border punch along bottom edge.
4. Trim with small punched dots and a strip of patterned paper. Adhere the top of the apron to the dress waist.
5. Cut waist band from coordinating patterned paper and adhere. Knot a short length of coordinating ribbon and adhere to side of apron. Tie to package.

Grandma's Zucchini Bread

Apron Tag

Christmas wouldn't be Christmas without the wonderful flavor of peppermint. Showcase Peppermint Bark Brownies in a red-and-white striped box. A candy sleigh full of Snowy Trail Mix makes a sweet ride! Rich and creamy Maine Maple Candies line up inside Paper Poppers for a holiday surprise.

Peppermint Bark Brownies

These brownies are welcome at any holiday occasion! Everyone loves chocolate and peppermint at Christmas!

20-oz. pkg. fudge brownie mix
12-oz. pkg. white chocolate chips
2 t. butter
¾ c. candy canes, crushed

Prepare and bake brownie mix according to package directions, using a greased 13"x9" baking pan. After baking, set aside and cool completely in pan, about one to 2 hours. In a saucepan over very low heat, melt chocolate chips and butter, stirring constantly with a rubber spatula. Spread chocolate mixture over brownies; sprinkle with crushed candy. Let stand for about 30 minutes, until frosting is hardened. Cut into squares. Makes 2 dozen.

Angie Biggin
Lyons, IL

Peppermint Bark Brownies
See-Through Brownie Box

See-Through Brownie Box instructions are on page 134.

Snowy Trail Mix
Candy Sleigh Holder

Maine Maple Candies
Paper Poppers

Snowy Trail Mix

So easy and so yummy! I have given it in little cellophane bags tied with a cute ribbon for gifts…everybody loves them.

3 c. mini pretzel sticks
1 1/2 c. bite-size corn & rice cereal
    squares
3/4 c. pecan halves
1/2 c. sweetened dried cranberries
1/2 c. cashew halves
1 c. red and green candy-coated
    chocolates
12-oz. pkg. white melting
    chocolate, chopped

In a large microwave-safe bowl, mix together all ingredients except white chocolate; set aside. Place white chocolate in a separate microwave-safe bowl. Microwave chocolate on high for one to 2 minutes; stir until smooth. Slowly pour melted chocolate over pretzel mixture, gently stirring until evenly coated. Scoop out onto wax paper. Let cool 20 minutes; break into bite-size clusters. Makes 10 cups.

Heather Plasterer
Colorado Springs, CO

Maine Maple Candies

These arrived as a Christmas surprise from my granny in Maine…what a yummy treat!

14-oz. can sweetened condensed
    milk
1/4 c. butter, softened
2 T. maple flavoring
1 1/2 c. chopped nuts
32-oz. pkg. powdered sugar
3 8-oz. pkgs. semi-sweet
    chocolate, chopped

Mix together condensed milk, butter, flavoring and nuts; gradually beat in powdered sugar. Roll into one-inch balls; refrigerate until ready to dip. Melt chocolate in a heavy saucepan over low heat; dip balls into chocolate. Place on wax paper-lined baking sheets until set. Keep refrigerated. Makes about 4 1/2 dozen.

Jennifer Martineau
Delaware, OH

Candy Sleigh Holder and Paper Poppers instructions are on page 135.

Country Herb Spread and Crispy Wheat Crackers stack up for a savory treat. Give spicy Pretzels with Pizzazz in a jar that can be used after the treats are gone. Orange-Macadamia Fudge, nestled in a festive tin, is the perfect gift for the sweet-tooth on your list!

Country Herb Spread

For variety, omit chives and dill; add one teaspoon fresh oregano and 1/2 teaspoon each fresh thyme, basil and marjoram.

8-oz. pkg. cream cheese, softened
1 T. mayonnaise
1 t. Dijon mustard
1 T. fresh chives, chopped
1 T. fresh dill, chopped
1 clove garlic, pressed
crackers

Combine all ingredients except crackers; stir until well blended. Serve with crackers. Makes 1 1/2 cups.

Cindy Brown
Farmington Hills, MI

Crispy Wheat Crackers

So delicious in soups and stews… terrific topped with cheese too!

1 3/4 c. whole-wheat flour
1 1/2 c. all-purpose flour
1 t. salt
1/3 c. oil
1 c. water
coarse salt to taste

In a medium bowl, combine flours and salt. Add oil and water, mixing until just blended. Roll dough out on a lightly floured surface to a thickness no greater than 1/8 inch. Place dough on an ungreased baking sheet; score squares with a knife without cutting through. Prick each square with a fork several times and sprinkle with salt. Bake at 350 degrees for 25 to 30 minutes, until crisp and golden. Allow crackers to cool on baking sheet. Remove and break into individual crackers. Makes 32 servings.

Country Herb Spread
Crispy Wheat Crackers
Gift Box

For You

Country Herb Spread Gift Box instructions are on page 135.

74 Gifts from the Country Kitchen

Pretzels with Pizzazz
Decorated Pretzel Jar

Pretzels with Pizzazz

Our family loves to watch sports on television…football, basketball, baseball…we love them all! These spicy pretzels are one of our favorite game-time or anytime snacks.

24-oz. pkg. mini twist pretzels
1 c. oil
2 T. red pepper flakes
1-oz. pkg. ranch salad dressing mix
2 T. grated Parmesan cheese
2 t. Italian seasoning

Transfer pretzels to a one-gallon container with a tight-fitting lid. Combine remaining ingredients in a bowl. Whisk until well mixed and pour over pretzels. Put lid on container and rotate until well coated, about 2 to 3 minutes. Let stand overnight before serving…if you can wait that long! Makes 20 to 24 servings.

Beckie Apple
Grannis, AR

Orange-Macadamia Fudge

A delicious way to let someone know you're thinking of them.

$^1/_2$ c. butter, melted
1 c. sugar
5-oz. can evaporated milk
2 c. mini marshmallows
1 c. semi-sweet chocolate chips
$^3/_4$ c. chopped macadamia nuts
1 t. orange extract

Combine butter, sugar and milk in a medium microwave-safe bowl; microwave on high for 5 minutes. Immediately add marshmallows and chocolate chips, stirring until pretzels are melted and smooth. Stir in nuts and orange extract. Pour into an 8"x 8" pan lined with aluminum foil; chill until firm. Remove fudge from pan, peel away foil and cut into squares. Store in refrigerator. Makes about 2 pounds.

Decorated Pretzel Jar and Candy Tin instructions are on pages 135 and 136.

Orange-Macadamia Fudge
Candy Tin

Homemade Graham Crackers

Make a S'mores gift basket and pack these up with chocolate bars and marshmallows...yum!

1/2 c. butter
3/4 c. brown sugar, packed
1 t. vanilla extract
2 c. whole-wheat flour
1 c. all-purpose flour
1 t. baking powder
1/2 t. baking soda
1/8 t. salt
1/2 c. milk

In a medium bowl, beat together butter and brown sugar with an electric mixer on medium speed; stir in vanilla. In a separate bowl, combine flours, baking powder, baking soda and salt; stir into butter mixture alternating with milk, beating with an electric mixer at medium speed until dough comes together and forms a ball. Divide dough in half and form into 2 discs; wrap tightly and chill one hour.

On a lightly floured surface, roll dough to 1/8-inch thickness; cut into 4-inch by 2-inch rectangles. Place each cracker 1/2 inch apart on parchment-lined baking sheets. Bake at 350 degrees for 12 to 14 minutes, until edges are golden. Remove crackers from baking sheets to cool on wire racks. Makes 30.

Spicy Fruit Tea Mix

This flavorful treat is great hot or cold.

20-oz. container orange drink mix
1 c. sugar
1 c. unsweetened instant tea mix
1/2 c. sweetened lemonade drink mix
1/4-oz. pkg. sweetened raspberry-flavored drink mix
2 t. cinnamon
1 t. nutmeg

Combine all ingredients; mix well. Store in an airtight container. Attach instructions. Makes 5 1/2 cups mix.

Instructions on card: Stir 2 tablespoons mix into one cup of hot or cold water. Makes one serving.

S'mores Container and Tea Jar Instructions are on page 136.

Homemade Graham Crackers
S'mores Container

Spicy Fruit Tea Mix
Tea Jar

Homemade Graham Crackers are a special gift and make the yummiest S'mores! A wonderful combination of flavors comes together for a warm-all-over Spicy Fruit Tea Mix that makes a perfect holiday gift. Add a little spice to a traditional favorite when you make Cinnamon Peanut Brittle. What a treat!

Cinnamon Peanut Brittle

I make this simple recipe every year for Christmas, and it's a huge hit...you'll never eat ordinary peanut brittle again!

1 c. sugar
1/2 c. light corn syrup
2 c. salted peanuts
1 t. butter
1/2 t. cinnamon
1 t. baking soda
1 t. vanilla extract

Combine sugar and corn syrup in a 2-quart microwave-safe glass container. Microwave, uncovered, on high for 4 minutes; stir. Heat 3 minutes longer; stir in peanuts, butter and cinnamon. Cook, uncovered, on high for 30 to 60 seconds, until mixture turns a light amber color. Mixture will be very hot. Quickly stir in baking soda and vanilla until light and foamy. Immediately pour onto a greased baking sheet and spread with a metal spatula. Refrigerate for 20 minutes, or until firm; break into pieces. Store in an airtight container. Makes 1 1/4 pounds.

Jennifer Oglesby
Brownsville, IN

Cinnamon Peanut Brittle Candy Pail

Candy Pail

- clear plastic pail with metal lid/ handle
- 2-3 coordinated patterned papers and cardstock
- cardstock border strips
- circle cutter or template
- fine-tipped liquid paint pen
- ball chain
- strong tape adhesive
- small hole punch
- corner rounder
- small tag die or punch
- ribbon and twine
- stamps, rub-on letters or computer/printer

1. Adhere a circle cut from patterned paper to the lid. Wrap a cardstock border strip around the middle of the pail and adhere with tape adhesive.

2. Print or stamp "Cinnamon Peanut Brittle" on white cardstock, trim to fit inside border and adhere.

3. **For tag:** Cut a rectangle from double-sided patterned paper and fold in half to create a small tag. Round corners and punch a small hole in the top. Die cut a small tag from coordinating cardstock. Print or stamp "Sweets for the Sweet" on white cardstock and adhere to the tag base. Add ribbon and twine to tag. Hang on the pail with ball chain.

Make-Ahead Brunch

Gathering together with family & friends is one of the best things about Christmas! Make your holiday brunch easier this year by stirring up Make-Ahead Pumpkin Pie French Toast and Sour Cream Streusel Coffee Cake. Be sure to try Grammy's Overnight Pancakes and Apple Pancake Syrup…the breakfast crowd will love them. And with all the time you've saved by using make-ahead recipes, you'll have time for a cup of coffee and one of Iva's Cinnamon Rolls!

Grammy's Overnight Pancakes

Whenever we visit Grammy, these yummy pancakes are on the breakfast table without fail. Usually they're surrounded by sausage or bacon, scrambled eggs and toast with jam. We can't imagine breakfast any other way!

2 c. long-cooking oats, uncooked
2 c. plus $^1/_4$ c. buttermilk, divided
$^1/_2$ c. all-purpose flour
$^1/_2$ c. whole-wheat flour
2 t. sugar
1 $^1/_2$ t. baking powder
1 $^1/_2$ t. baking soda
1 t. salt
2 eggs
2 T. butter, melted and cooled
oil for frying
Apple Pancake Syrup

Combine oats and 2 cups buttermilk in a bowl; cover and refrigerate overnight.

To prepare pancakes, stir together flours, sugar, baking powder, baking soda and salt. Set aside.

In a large bowl, beat together eggs and butter. Stir into oat mixture. Add flour mixture, stirring well. If batter is too thick, stir in 2 to 4 tablespoons remaining buttermilk. Pour batter by $^1/_4$ cupfuls onto a well-greased hot griddle. Cook until bubbles appear on the surface; flip and cook other side until golden. Top with Apple Pancake Syrup. Makes 16.

Regina Ferrigno
Gooseberry Patch

Grammy's Overnight Pancakes
Apple Pancake Syrup

Apple Pancake Syrup

My older sister, Teena, often cooked for my siblings and me. She would make this syrup to serve on our breakfast pancakes and waffles...she could really make something from nothing!

6-oz. can frozen sugar-free apple
   juice concentrate, thawed
$^3/_4$ c. water
$^1/_2$ t. lemon juice
1 T. cornstarch
$^1/_4$ t. cinnamon

Mix all ingredients in a saucepan. Cook over medium heat, stirring frequently, until thickened and reduced by half, about 15 minutes. Serves 4 to 6.

Gail Shepard
Missoula, MT

79

Heat & Hold Scrambled Eggs

Serve with a stack of buttered toast and a platter of sizzling sausage…yum!

1 doz. eggs, beaten
1 1/3 c. milk
1 t. salt
1/8 t. pepper
2 T. all-purpose flour
1 T. pimento, chopped
1 T. fresh parsley, chopped
1/4 c. butter

Combine all ingredients except butter in a large bowl. Whisk until smooth; set aside. Melt butter in a large skillet over low heat; pour egg mixture into skillet. Cook and stir until eggs are desired consistency. Can be held for up to one hour in chafing dish or an electric skillet set at 200 degrees. Serves 6.

Judy Collins
Nashville, TN

Farmhouse Sausage Patties

Adding your own special ingredients to plain sausage really makes it taste terrific. It's great crumbled for sausage gravy or shaped into patties with eggs and toast for a real country breakfast.

1 lb. ground pork
1 t. ground cumin
1/2 t. dried thyme
1/2 t. dried sage
1 t. salt
1/2 t. pepper
Optional: 1/8 t. cayenne pepper

Combine all ingredients; mix well. Cover and refrigerate overnight to allow flavors to blend. Form into six 3-inch or twelve 1 1/2-inch patties. Arrange in a lightly greased skillet and brown both sides over medium heat. Serves 6.

Heat & Hold Scrambled Eggs Farmhouse Sausage Patties

Sour Cream Streusel Coffee Cake

Sour Cream Streusel Coffee Cake

This sweet, nutty coffee cake can be made a day ahead…what a time saver for busy hostesses! Cool completely, then wrap in aluminum foil and store at room temperature.

1¼ c. walnuts, coarsely chopped
1¼ c. brown sugar, packed
4½ t. cinnamon
4½ t. baking cocoa
3 c. cake flour
1½ t. baking powder
1½ t. baking soda
¾ t. salt
¾ c. butter, softened
1½ c. sugar
3 eggs
1 T. vanilla extract
6-oz. container sour cream
1 c. powdered sugar
1 T. milk

Mix walnuts, brown sugar, cinnamon and cocoa in a small bowl; set aside. Sift flour, baking powder, baking soda and salt into a medium bowl; set aside. With an electric mixer on medium speed, beat butter and sugar in a large bowl. Beat in eggs, one at a time; mix in vanilla. Add flour mixture and sour cream alternately into butter mixture in 3 additions; beat on high speed for one minute. Pour ⅓ of batter into a buttered 12-cup Bundt® pan; sprinkle with half of nut mixture. Spoon remaining batter over top. Bake at 350 degrees until a toothpick inserted near center comes out clean, about one hour. Cool cake in pan on a wire rack for 10 minutes; run a knife around pan sides to loosen. Turn cake out onto rack and cool for one hour. Transfer to a serving platter. Whisk powdered sugar and milk together in a small bowl and drizzle over cake. May be served warm or at room temperature. Serves 8 to 10.

Kathy Terry
Delaware, OH

Iva's Cinnamon Rolls

When I first met my husband's Grandma, Iva, she instantly accepted me as her own granddaughter! She showed me how to make these yummy cinnamon rolls…anyone can pass on a recipe, but to watch how a recipe is artfully put together is priceless.

.75-oz. pkg. active dry yeast
2 c. very warm water, divided
1 c. shortening
2 eggs, beaten
1 c. sugar
1 T. salt
6½ c. all-purpose flour
6 T. butter, softened
½ c. brown sugar, packed
1 T. cinnamon

Dissolve yeast in ¼ cup of very warm water, 110 to 115 degrees. In a separate bowl, combine shortening and remaining water; set aside. Mix together shortening mixture, eggs, sugar and salt. Add yeast mixture to shortening mixture; stir in flour. Turn dough into a greased bowl (dough will be soft); cover with a tea towel. Let rise in a warm place (85 degrees), free from drafts until double in size, about 2 hours; punch down dough. Divide dough into 2 parts. Roll each part into an 18-inch by 13-inch rectangle on a floured surface. Spread butter over surface. Sprinkle evenly with brown sugar and cinnamon, adding more to taste if desired. Roll up, starting on one long side; cut one-inch-thick slices. Place into 2 greased 13"x 9" or 10" round baking pans. Cover; let rise for 45 minutes, until double in size. Bake at 375 degrees for about 25 minutes. Cool and spread with Frosting. Makes 2½ dozen.

Frosting:

4 c. powdered sugar
¼ c. butter, softened
1 T. to ¼ c. milk

Combine powdered sugar and butter; add milk to desired consistency. Makes 1¾ cup.

Bobbi Janssen
Lanark, IL

If your gang has worked up an appetite opening presents, they'll love Heat & Hold Scrambled Eggs with Farmhouse Sausage Patties. Need a little something sweet? Everyone will enjoy a thick slice of Sour Cream Streusel Coffee Cake! Bake some of Iva's Cinnamon Rolls and you'll find everyone coming to the kitchen!

Iva's Cinnamon Rolls

You'll be calm and collected on Christmas morning because you stirred up Make-Ahead Pumpkin Pie French Toast the night before! Using store-bought biscuits makes the Smith Family Breakfast Bake so easy to prepare…just be sure to make plenty!

Make-Ahead Pumpkin Pie French Toast

Make-Ahead Pumpkin Pie French Toast

I combined several different French toast recipes to suit my family's tastes. They love anything with pumpkin, so the pumpkin pie spice was a must. It's a great Sunday morning breakfast. Or, it can bake while you get ready for church. It's also super-easy for husbands to whip up so Mom can sleep in just a bit on Saturday morning!

1 loaf French, Italian, challah
    or Hawaiian bread, cut into
    1-inch slices
3 eggs, beaten
1/2 c. egg substitute
1 c. half-and-half
1 1/2 c. milk
1/4 t. salt
1 t. vanilla extract
1 T. pumpkin pie spice
1/2 c. brown sugar, packed
1 to 2 T. butter, sliced

Arrange bread slices in the bottom of a greased 13"x9" baking pan. Whisk together eggs, egg substitute, half-and-half, milk, salt, vanilla and spice. Stir in brown sugar; pour mixture over bread slices. Refrigerate, covered, overnight. Dot top with butter and bake, uncovered, at 350 degrees for 40 to 45 minutes. Serves 8.

Jennifer Yandle
Indian Trail, NC

Creamy Crock Hashbrowns

I like to serve this yummy side with grilled ham slices. The recipe can easily be halved for a smaller group, but don't underestimate how many people will ask for seconds!

32-oz. pkg. frozen diced potatoes
16-oz. container sour cream
10 3/4-oz. can cream of celery
    soup
10 3/4-oz. can cream of chicken
    soup
1 onion, chopped
2 T. butter, melted
1/4 t. pepper
2 c. shredded sharp Cheddar
    cheese

Place potatoes in a 5-quart slow cooker. Combine remaining ingredients; pour over potatoes. Stir to mix well. Cover and cook on low setting for 5 to 6 hours. Serves 10 to 12.

Diane Cohen
The Woodlands, TX

Smith Family Breakfast Bake

I created this recipe to duplicate one that I tasted and loved. Now my kids and husband love it too!

12-oz. tube refrigerated biscuits,
    baked and torn
1 lb. ground pork sausage,
    browned and drained
8 eggs, beaten
2 c. milk
1 sprig fresh rosemary, chopped
1 t. Italian seasoning
1 t. dried basil
1 t. dried oregano
1 t. dried thyme
salt and pepper to taste
8-oz. pkg. shredded Cheddar
    cheese

Arrange torn biscuits in a lightly greased 13"x9" baking pan. Top with sausage; set aside. Blend eggs and milk with seasonings. Pour over sausage; sprinkle with cheese. Bake, uncovered, at 350 degrees for 30 minutes, or until golden. Serves 12.

Cherylann Smith
Efland, NC

Smith Family Breakfast Bake

Winter Fruit Salad

Perfect to make during the winter months when fresh fruit is not as abundant. It can be made a day ahead for a holiday brunch.

$^1/_2$ c. sugar
2 T. cornstarch
20-oz. can pineapple chunks,
    drained and $^3/_4$ c. juice
    reserved
$^1/_3$ c. orange juice
1 T. lemon juice
11-oz. can mandarin oranges,
    drained
3 to 4 red and green apples,
    cored and chopped
2 to 3 bananas, sliced

In a saucepan, combine sugar and cornstarch. Add reserved pineapple juice, orange juice and lemon juice. Cook and stir over medium heat until thick and bubbly; cook and stir one minute longer. Remove from heat; set aside. In a bowl, combine pineapple, oranges, apples and bananas. Pour warm sauce over fruit; stir gently to coat. Cover and refrigerate before serving. Serves 12.

Nancy Girard
Chesapeake, VA

Traditional Christmas Eve Dinner

The night before Christmas brings so many wonderful memories....carolers, wrapping last-minute gifts and sitting down to the table to have Christmas Eve dinner with the family. Prepare a baked ham to be the showpiece of your dinner. Then add savory vegetables full of flavor. Still waiting on a few of the guests to arrive? Satisfy hungry appetites with a sampling of Bruschetta with Cranberry Relish. You'll be replenishing the bread basket over and over when you fill it with Cloverleaf Oat Rolls fresh from the oven. And everyone will save room for your holiday dessert, Eggnog Pound Cake. Make this Christmas Eve a magical night with recipes that are sure to please.

Ham with Cumberland Sauce

Ham with Cumberland Sauce

It's the fruity sauce that makes this ham special. Named after the Duke of Cumberland, the sauce was actually created in Germany... you're going to love it!

9 to 10-lb. fully-cooked bone-in
    ham
1/2 c. brown sugar, packed
1 t. dry mustard
1 to 2 t. whole cloves
Garnish: fresh currants, fresh
    thyme and sage

Using a sharp knife, score ham in diamond shapes. In a medium bowl, combine brown sugar and mustard; spread over ham. Insert a whole clove in center of each diamond. Place ham in a large roaster with a rack. Bake, uncovered, at 325 degrees for 20 to 22 minutes per pound, about one hour and 40 minutes, or until ham is heated through and meat thermometer reads 140 degrees. Garnish with fresh currants, thyme and sage. Serve with Cumberland Sauce. Serves 8 to 10.

Cumberland Sauce:

12-oz. jar red currant or apple
    jelly
1/4 c. orange juice
1/4 c. lemon juice
1/4 c. red wine or apple juice
2 T. honey
1 T. cornstarch

Combine ingredients in a medium saucepan. Cook over medium heat until sauce thickens, stirring often. Makes 1 3/4 cups.

Geneva Rogers
Gillette, WY

85

Add a fresh flavor twist when you serve Bruschetta with Cranberry Relish. They'll love their veggies when you serve Roasted Walnut & Pear Salad and Harvest Vegetables at your holiday meal.

Bruschetta with Cranberry Relish

Serve these crisp, savory slices at your next holiday feast…you may just start a new tradition!

1 French baguette loaf, sliced
    1/4-inch thick
1 to 2 T. olive oil
1 t. orange zest
1 t. lemon zest
1/2 c. chopped pecans
1/2 c. crumbled blue cheese

Brush baguette slices lightly with oil. Arrange on a broiler pan; toast lightly under broiler. Turn slices over; spread with Cranberry Relish. Sprinkle with zests, pecans and blue cheese. Place under broiler just until cheese begins to melt. Makes 18 to 20 appetizer servings.

Cranberry Relish:
16-oz. can whole-berry cranberry
    sauce
6-oz. pkg. sweetened dried
    cranberries
1/2 c. sugar
1 t. rum extract
1 c. chopped pecans

Stir all ingredients together.

Rhonda Johnson
Studio City, CA

Bruschetta with Cranberry Relish

Roasted Walnut & Pear Salad

This is wonderful for a formal dinner or a casual warm family gathering. Be sure to use fresh pears for the best flavor.

1 head romaine lettuce, torn
2 c. pears, thinly sliced
2 Roma tomatoes, chopped
1 c. walnuts
2 T. butter
1/4 c. brown sugar, packed
4-oz. pkg. crumbled blue cheese
8-oz. bottle raspberry white wine
    salad dressing

Place lettuce in a large serving bowl; lay pears on top and add tomatoes. In a medium skillet, toast walnuts in butter until golden; add brown sugar and stir over low heat until walnuts are hardened with glaze. Add walnuts to salad, sprinkle blue cheese and toss with desired amount of vinegar dressing. Serves 6 to 8.

Laurie Johnson
Rosenberg, TX

Harvest Vegetables

Harvest Vegetables

Roasted and slightly garlicky in flavor, these vegetables are everyone's favorites!

2 lbs. butternut squash, halved,
    seeded and cut into 1^1/$_2$-inch
    cubes
2 lbs. redskin potatoes, quartered
2 to 3 red onions, quartered
16-oz. pkg. baby carrots
4 to 6 cloves garlic, crushed
3 T. olive oil, divided
2 t. coarse salt, divided
^{1}/$_4$ t. pepper, divided

Combine vegetables and garlic; spread evenly onto 2 lightly greased baking sheets. Toss with oil, salt and pepper. Bake at 450 degrees for 40 to 50 minutes, tossing vegetables and rotating sheets from top to bottom of oven halfway through. Serve hot or at room temperature. Serves 8.

Jo Ann

Creamy Bacon & Herb Succotash

You'll love this deluxe version of an old harvest-time favorite...I do!

^{1}/$_4$ lb. bacon, chopped
1 onion, diced
10-oz. pkg. frozen lima beans
^{1}/$_2$ c. water
salt and pepper to taste
10-oz. pkg. frozen corn
^{1}/$_2$ c. whipping cream
1^1/$_2$ t. fresh thyme, minced
Garnish: 2 t. fresh chives, snipped

In a Dutch oven over medium-high heat, cook bacon until crisp. Remove bacon, reserving 2 tablespoons drippings in Dutch oven. Add onion; sauté until tender, about 5 minutes. Add beans, water, salt and pepper; bring to a boil. Reduce heat; cover and simmer for 5 minutes. Stir in corn, cream and thyme; return to a simmer. Cook until vegetables are tender, about 5 minutes. Toss with reserved bacon and chives before serving. Serves 6.

Vickie

Roasted Walnut & Pear Salad

Quick-cooking oats and brown sugar are the secret to Cloverleaf Oat Rolls…just add a pat of butter and enjoy! Bits of flaked coconut make Eggnog Pound Cake the perfect holiday dessert. Dress up the cake with red berry sprinkles.

Cloverleaf Oat Rolls

Cloverleaf Oat Rolls

It wouldn't be dinner at Grandma's without a basket of her delicious homemade rolls on the dinner table!

1 c. quick-cooking oats, uncooked
$^1/_3$ c. brown sugar, packed
1 t. salt
$^1/_3$ c. shortening
1 $^1/_2$ c. boiling water, divided
1 env. active dry yeast
4 c. all-purpose flour, divided
1 egg, beaten

Place oats, brown sugar, salt and shortening in a large bowl; pour 1 $^1/_4$ cups boiling water over all. Let stand until lukewarm. In a separate small bowl, let remaining water cool slightly (110 to 115 degrees); sprinkle with yeast and stir until dissolved. Add yeast mixture to oat mixture along with 2 cups flour and egg. Beat until well blended. Add remaining flour, a little at a time, to make a soft dough. Turn onto a lightly floured surface; knead until smooth and elastic. Place dough in a greased bowl; turn so top is greased. Cover with a tea towel; let rise in a warm place until double in bulk, about 1 $^1/_2$ hours. Punch down; let rise again until double, about 30 minutes. Form into one-inch balls; place 3 balls in each cup of greased muffin tins. Let rise again until double, 20 to 30 minutes. Bake at 375 degrees for about 25 minutes, until golden. Makes about 2 $^1/_2$ dozen.

Sharon Cinder
Junction City, KS

Spinach Soufflé

Use Swiss cheese instead of Cheddar if you like.

10-oz. pkg. frozen, chopped
    spinach, thawed
3 T. all-purpose flour
3 eggs, beaten
$^1/_2$ t. salt
12-oz. carton cottage cheese
$^1/_2$ c. shredded Cheddar cheese
$^1/_4$ c. butter, melted

In a large mixing bowl, combine spinach and flour; add eggs, salt, cottage cheese, Cheddar cheese and butter. Place in a greased 13" x 9" baking dish. Bake, covered, at 375 degrees for 45 minutes. Uncover and bake an additional 15 minutes. Serves 6.

Gloria Robertson
Midland, TX

Eggnog Pound Cake

This is a cake that reminds me of sweet Christmases and favorite family gatherings.

1 c. butter, softened
1 c. shortening
3 c. sugar
6 eggs
3 c. all-purpose flour
1 c. eggnog
1 t. lemon extract
1 t. vanilla extract
1 t. coconut extract
1 c. sweetened flaked coconut
Garnish: edible glitter, red berry
    sprinkles

Blend together butter and shortening using an electric mixer on medium speed. Gradually add sugar; beat until fluffy. Add eggs, one at a time, beating well after each addition. Use a spoon to stir in flour alternately with eggnog. Blend in extracts and coconut.

Pour into a greased and floured 10" Bundt® pan. Bake at 325 degrees for 1 1/2 hours; cool for 10 minutes before removing from pan. Cool completely before spreading with Spice Frosting. Garnish with edible glitter and red berry sprinkles. Serves 12 to 14.

Spice Frosting:
2 T. butter, softened
2 oz. cream cheese, softened
2 c. powdered sugar
3 T. milk
1/8 t. cinnamon
pinch nutmeg

Blend together butter and cream cheese until smooth. Gradually add sugar alternately with milk; beat until smooth. Blend in cinnamon and nutmeg.

Nancy Cohrs
Donna, TX

Tennessee Fudge Pie

My mama has always made this pie for holiday meals ... people request it for church socials, parties and family suppers. It's a chocolate lover's dream!

2 eggs, beaten
1/2 c. butter, melted and cooled
1/4 c. baking cocoa
1/4 c. all-purpose flour
1 c. sugar
2 t. vanilla extract
1/3 c. semi-sweet chocolate chips
1/3 c. chopped pecans
9-inch pie crust

Beat together eggs and butter in a large bowl. Add remaining ingredients except pie crust; mix well. Pour into pie crust. Bake at 350 degrees for 25 minutes, or until center is firm. Serves 8.

Dusty Jones
Paxton, IL

Eggnog Pound Cake

Need to add a little variety to your holiday meal plans this year? Think nuts! Yes, nuts not only add a tasty flavor and wonderful texture to many dishes…they are also good for you! So try a hearty Crispy Pecan-Chicken Casserole rich with cheese and sour cream. Or set out the crackers and serve Almond-Bacon Spread for that special party. Simple to make and oh-so-chocolatey, Tiny Turtle Cupcakes will be the hit of the day. So gather up the cashews, almonds and pecans and enjoy being nuts about nuts!

Nuts
ABOUT
♥ NUTS ♥

Crispy Pecan-Chicken Casserole

Crispy Pecan-Chicken Casserole

This creamy casserole is fast and fantastic!

2 c. cooked chicken, chopped
$^1/_2$ c. chopped pecans
2 T. onion, finely chopped
$^3/_4$ c. celery, sliced
1 c. mayonnaise
$^1/_2$ c. sour cream
$10^3/_4$-oz. can cream of chicken
   soup
2 t. lemon juice
1 c. potato chips, crushed
1 c. shredded Cheddar cheese

   Mix together all ingredients except chips and cheese. Place in a lightly greased 3-quart casserole dish. Combine chips and cheese; sprinkle on top. Bake, uncovered, at 375 degrees for 30 to 35 minutes, until golden and bubbly. Serves 6.

Michelle Greeley
Hayes, VA

Rich cashews add that special crunch to a wonderful Apricot-Cashew Salad. Serve on bread or on a lettuce leaf for a tasty treat. Need a quick dish for a holiday event? Stir up Tropical Chicken Stir-Fry and serve with fresh fruit for a yummy and satisfying meal.

Apricot-Cashew Salad

So versatile…the kids enjoy this for lunch as a wrap or sandwich, but I've also served it over red leaf lettuce for a ladies' luncheon at church.

2 c. cooked turkey, diced
1 Granny Smith apple, cored, peeled and diced
1 c. celery, chopped
1/4 c. dried apricots, finely chopped
1/2 c. cashews, chopped
1/2 c. mayonnaise
1/4 c. sour cream
2 T. apricot preserves
1/4 t. ground ginger
1/8 t. nutmeg
1/8 t. pepper
8 slices sandwich bread
4 lettuce leaves

In a large bowl, toss together turkey, apple, celery, apricots and cashews; set aside. In a separate bowl, whisk together remaining ingredients; spoon over turkey mixture and fold in until well blended. Spoon evenly onto 4 slices of bread. Top with a lettuce leaf and remaining bread slices. Serves 4.

Rhonda Reeder
Ellicott City, MD

Apricot-Cashew Salad

Tropical Chicken Stir-Fry

*This dish is so yummy and cooks up in a jiffy…
it's a little taste of the islands! I like to serve
scoops of orange sherbet and coconut ice
cream for a sweet end to dinner.*

1/4 c. soy sauce
2 T. sugar
1 T. cider vinegar
1 T. catsup
1 T. garlic, minced
1 t. cornstarch
1/2 t. ground ginger
8-oz. can pineapple chunks,
    drained and 1/4 c. juice
    reserved
2 T. oil

1 lb. boneless, skinless chicken
    breasts, sliced into strips
16-oz. pkg. frozen stir-fry
    vegetables, thawed
cooked rice
sliced almonds, toasted

In a bowl, mix first 7 ingredients
and reserved pineapple juice; set
aside. Heat oil in a skillet over
medium-high heat. Add chicken;
cook and stir for 5 minutes, until
nearly done. Add vegetables; cook
and stir for 4 minutes. Stir in
pineapple and soy sauce mixture;
heat through. Serve over cooked
rice; sprinkle with almonds.
Serves 6.

Vickie

Tropical Chicken Stir-Fry

You can't spread it on too thick! Not when you are serving Almond-Bacon Spread…sure to become everyone's asked-for cracker topper. Oh-so-gooey and yummy, Tiny Turtle Cupcakes are a treat at the end of a holiday meal or anytime! Make some extras to give as sweet little gifts.

Almond-Bacon Spread
This is a very old recipe that I've used for many years.

$1/4$ c. roasted almonds, finely
    chopped
2 slices bacon, crisply cooked and
    crumbled
1 c. shredded American or sharp
    Cheddar cheese
1 T. green onion, chopped
$1/2$ c. mayonnaise
$1/8$ t. salt
crackers or sliced party rye

Stir together all ingredients except crackers or bread in a bowl until thoroughly combined. Serve with crackers or sliced party rye. Serves 6.

Joan Clark
Cortland, OH

Almond-Bacon Spread

Tiny Turtle Cupcakes

I give these little chocolate bites to my kids' soccer coaches for an end-of-the-season gift…and keep some for myself, too!

2 1/2-oz. pkg. brownie mix
1/2 c. pecans, chopped
16-oz. container chocolate
    frosting
1/2 c. pecans, toasted and
    coarsely chopped

Prepare brownie batter according to package directions. Stir in chopped pecans. Fill paper-lined mini muffin cups 2/3 full. Bake at 350 degrees for 18 minutes, or until a toothpick tests clean. Cool cupcakes in tins on wire racks 5 minutes. Remove from tins; cool completely. Frost cupcakes; top with toasted pecans. Spoon Caramel Sauce evenly over cupcakes. Store in refrigerator. Makes 4 1/2 dozen.

Caramel Sauce:
12 caramels, unwrapped
1 to 2 T. whipping cream

Combine caramels and one tablespoon cream in a small saucepan; cook and stir over low heat until smooth. Add remaining cream as needed for desired consistency.

Teresa Podracky
Solon, OH

Tiny Turtle Cupcakes

95

Satisfying Soups and Sandwiches

Share those wonderful Christmas evenings together with a warm bowl of homemade soup or a tasty sandwich. Try adding a little spice to the gathering by stirring up some Poblano Chowder or Grandma Hallie's Spicy Chili. While the soup is simmering on the stove or in the slow cooker, you can wrap those last-minute presents and listen to Christmas carols. To make the meal complete, add a Cobb Sandwich layered with all the fixings! No matter which soup or sandwich you try, you'll feel warm and toasty as you share the holiday together.

Buffalo Chicken Wing Soup

This spicy, creamy soup warms you up from your toes to your nose on a cold winter day!

6 c. milk
3 10³/₄-oz. cans cream of
    chicken soup
3 c. chicken, cooked and shredded
1 c. sour cream
¹/₄ to ¹/₂ c. hot pepper sauce
Garnish: shredded Monterey Jack
    cheese, chopped green onions

Combine all ingredients except garnish in a 5-quart slow cooker. Cover and cook on low setting for 4 to 5 hours. To serve, garnish with cheese and onions. Serves 8.

Anna McMaster
Portland, OR

Hearty Kielbasa & Kale Soup

This flavorful soup is rich and delicious.

8 oz. Kielbasa sausage, sliced
1 lb. kale, chopped and stems
    removed
1 onion, chopped
1 potato, cubed
3 cloves garlic, minced
2 14¹/₂-oz. cans chicken broth
15-oz. can Great Northern
    beans, rinsed and drained
1 t. dried thyme
1 t. pepper

In a medium stockpot over medium heat, cook Kielbasa, kale, onion, potato and garlic, stirring frequently until kale begins to wilt and sausage browns. Stir in the next 4 ingredients. Increase heat to high; bring to a boil. Reduce heat to medium; partially cover and simmer for 12 minutes, or until potatoes are tender.
Serves 6 to 8.

Kathy Royer
Charlotte, NC

Buffalo Chicken Wing Soup

Poblano Chowder

Invite the whole gang over for a soup supper and to watch a classic holiday movie! They will be asking for seconds of tangy Poblano Chowder as they cuddle up on the couch. Chili is a winter classic. This year, try Grandma Hallie's Spicy Chili for a new variety of this favorite soup! Serve it with a sandwich for a hearty winter meal.

Poblano Chowder

This is wonderful served with toasted Italian or French bread. I usually double the recipe and invite friends over to share it.

½ c. plus 2 T. butter or oil, divided
2 poblano peppers, diced
1 red onion, diced
8-oz. pkg. sliced mushrooms
½ c. all-purpose flour
4 c. chicken broth
2 to 3 potatoes, peeled and diced
1½ to 2 c. corn
3 tomatoes, diced
1 jalapeño pepper, diced
2 T. salt
1 T. pepper
1 T. garlic powder
2 c. heavy cream
Optional: 1 c. fresh cilantro, finely
    chopped
Garnish: cooked shrimp, crab,
    sausage, chicken or beef

Heat ¼ cup butter or oil in a Dutch oven over medium-high heat; add poblano peppers, onion and mushrooms. Cook 6 to 8 minutes, until vegetables are lightly browned. Add in flour, stirring until vegetables are coated. Add remaining ingredients except cilantro and garnish. Bring to a simmer. Reduce heat to low and simmer, uncovered, 20 minutes or until potatoes are tender. Sprinkle with cilantro and garnish, if desired. Serves 10.

Charlotte Bryant
Grayson, GA

Grandma Hallie's Spicy Chili

This recipe is from my Great-Grandma Hallie. I am so glad I actually have one of her recipes written down! She would make the best food and say, "Honey, it's all up here," meaning she memorized all her recipes. This recipe shows what a wonderful cook she was!

2 lbs. ground beef
$\frac{1}{4}$ c. dried, minced onion
2 t. salt
2 10$\frac{3}{4}$-oz. cans tomato soup
2 16-oz. cans kidney beans, rinsed and drained
2$\frac{1}{2}$ c. water
1 t. Worcestershire sauce
2 T. butter, sliced
3 T. chili powder
Garnish: sour cream, shredded Cheddar cheese, sliced green onion

Brown beef in a large pot over medium heat; drain. Add remaining ingredients except garnish; reduce heat to medium-low. Simmer for 45 minutes, stirring occasionally. Garnish as desired. Serves 8 to 10.

Ashley Hull
Virden, IL

Triple-Take Grilled Cheese

Delicious in winter with a steaming bowl of chili...scrumptious in summer made with produce fresh from the garden!

1 T. oil
8 slices sourdough bread
$\frac{1}{4}$ c. butter, softened and divided
4 slices white American cheese
4 slices Muenster cheese
$\frac{1}{2}$ c. shredded sharp Cheddar cheese
Optional: 4 slices red onion, 4 slices tomato, $\frac{1}{4}$ c. chopped fresh basil

Heat oil in a skillet over medium heat. Spread 2 bread slices with one tablespoon butter; place one slice butter-side down on skillet. Layer one slice American, one slice Muenster and 2 tablespoons Cheddar cheese on bread. If desired, top each with an onion slice, a tomato slice and one tablespoon basil. Butter 2 slices of bread; add to sandwiches in skillet. Reduce heat to medium-low. Cook until golden on one side, about 3 to 5 minutes; flip and cook until golden on the other side. Repeat with remaining ingredients. Makes 4 sandwiches.

Abigail Smith
Columbus, OH

Grandma Hallie's Spicy Chili
Triple-Take Grilled Cheese

Cobb Sandwiches

Everyone loves sandwiches! In no time you can make layered Cobb Sandwiches for everyone to enjoy! Or put together Henderson Family Gyros... they are sure to ask for more!

Cobb Sandwiches

If you don't have time to fry bacon, mix bacon bits with the blue cheese dressing.

2 T. blue cheese salad dressing
3 slices bread, toasted
4-oz. grilled boneless, skinless
   chicken breast
1 leaf green leaf lettuce
2 slices tomato
3 slices avocado
1 slice red onion
3 slices bacon, crisply cooked

Spread blue cheese dressing on one side of each slice of toasted bread. On the first slice of bread, place chicken breast on dressing; top with a second bread slice. Layer on lettuce, tomato, avocado, onion and bacon; top with remaining bread slice. Cut sandwich in quarters, securing each section with a toothpick. Makes 4 sandwich wedges.

Joyce Chizauskie
Vacaville, CA

Red Pepper & Chicken Bagels

This is a quick recipe that's perfect whenever time is short.

2 boneless, skinless chicken
   breasts
$1/8$ t. salt
$1/8$ t. pepper
$1/4$ c. balsamic vinegar
3 T. Worcestershire sauce
2 bagels, split
2 slices fresh mozzarella cheese
2 slices roasted red pepper

Place chicken between 2 pieces of wax paper; pound until thin. Sprinkle with salt and pepper. In a bowl, combine vinegar and Worcestershire sauce; marinate chicken 10 to 15 minutes. Drain and discard marinade. Place chicken on a lightly greased grill or in a skillet over medium heat. Cook and turn chicken until golden and juices run clear, about 20 minutes. Place chicken on bagel halves; top with cheese, pepper slices and remaining bagel halves. Arrange on an ungreased baking sheet and bake at 350 degrees until cheese is melted, about 5 to 10 minutes. Serves 2.

Janice Pigga
Bethlehem, PA

Henderson Family Gyros

This recipe marinates the meat for 6 to 12 hours. The result is worth it...meat that's tender and bursting with flavor!

1/4 c. olive oil
1/4 c. dry red wine or cranberry
　　juice cocktail
Optional: 1 T. vinegar
4 garlic cloves, chopped
1 T. fresh oregano, chopped
2 lbs. pork or turkey tenderloin,
　　thinly sliced
6 pita rounds, split
Garnish: baby spinach, red onion
　　slices, tomato slices

Combine oil, wine or juice and vinegar (only if using juice), garlic and oregano in a large plastic zipping bag. Add pork or turkey; seal and refrigerate 6 to 12 hours. Line grill surface with a piece of aluminum foil coated with non-stick vegetable spray. Heat grill to medium-high heat. Using a slotted spoon, remove meat mixture from plastic zipping bag and arrange on aluminum foil. Discard marinade. Grill and turn meat slices until browned. Drain and remove from grill. Toast pitas on grill until warmed. Spoon meat into pitas; drizzle with Cucumber Sauce. Top with desired amounts of spinach, onion and tomato. Serves 6.

Cucumber Sauce:

1/4 c. sour cream
1/4 c. cucumber, peeled and diced
2 T. red onion, minced
1/4 t. lemon pepper
1/4 t. dried oregano
1/8 t. garlic powder

Combine all ingredients in a bowl. Chill until ready to serve.

Jessica Henderson
Bloomfield, IA

Turkey & Black Bean Quesadillas

Perfect for those nights when everyone is busy with homework, meetings and rehearsal.

15-oz. can black beans, rinsed and
　　drained
6 oz. Cheddar cheese, cubed
4 oz. thinly sliced, cooked turkey,
　　cut into strips
1/2 c. salsa
8 8-inch flour tortillas
2 T. butter, melted
Garnish: sour cream and salsa

In a large mixing bowl, stir together beans, cheese, turkey and salsa. Brush one side of tortillas with butter. Place buttered side down on an ungreased baking sheet. Spoon about 1/3 cup bean mixture on half of each tortilla; fold in half. Bake at 375 degrees for 10 to 15 minutes, until heated through; let cool for 5 minutes. Cut each quesadilla into 3 wedges. Garnish with sour cream and salsa. Serves 4.

Jo Ann

Henderson Family Gyros

Cookies for Santa

Dropped, sliced, cut-outs or bars…'tis the season for Christmas cookies! Warm up the kids with some Sugar Cookie Mittens and a glass of milk. Be sure to make enough of Emily's Gingerbread Cookies for Santa this year as well as for the cookie exchange. Stack up a plate with Winslow Whoopie Pies and watch them disappear. For that pretty cookie you need to finish your holiday cookie tray, stir up some Blueberry Linzer Tarts…they'll be the show piece of the plate. So start baking these special little holiday treats for everyone you love. Santa will thank you!

Sugar Cookie Mittens

Sugar Cookie Mittens

Everybody needs a dependable cut-out cookie recipe for Christmas…this is mine! I collect cookie cutters and this works so well with them.

2 c. butter, softened
1⅓ c. sugar
2 eggs, beaten
2 t. vanilla extract
5 c. all-purpose flour

Blend butter and sugar together; stir in eggs and vanilla. Add flour; mix until well blended. Shape into a ball; cover and chill for 4 hours to overnight. Roll out dough ¼-inch thick on a lightly floured surface; cut out with cookie cutters as desired. Arrange cookies on lightly greased baking sheets. Bake at 350 degrees for 8 to 10 minutes, until golden. Frost cookies when cool. Makes 4 dozen.

Frosting:
4½ c. powdered sugar
6 T. butter, melted
6 T. milk
2 T. vanilla extract
1 T. lemon juice
Optional: few drops food coloring

Combine all ingredients in a medium bowl. Beat with an electric mixer on low speed until smooth.

Tina Knotts
Cable, OH

Grab the kids, frosting and colorful sprinkles and have some family fun creating Emily's Gingerbread Cookies. Each little member of the gingerbread family will have his or her own personality! Little bits of red cherries make Santa's Whiskers a sweet cookie that everyone will love.

Emily's Gingerbread Cookies

This came from my daughter Emily's elementary class assignment. She unscrambled words to uncover the recipe... she wrote "flower" instead of "flour." I still have the paper and treasure it!

1/3 c. brown sugar, packed
1/3 c. shortening
2/3 c. molasses
1 egg, beaten
3 c. all-purpose flour
1 T. baking powder
1 1/2 t. ground ginger
1/2 t. salt
Garnish: Frosting (page 103)

Blend together brown sugar and shortening until light and fluffy. Beat in molasses. Add egg, beating well. In a separate bowl, sift together flour, baking powder, ginger and salt. Add flour mixture to sugar mixture; mix well. Cover and refrigerate for 2 hours. Divide dough into fourths. Roll out to 1/4-inch thickness. Cut with cookie cutters. Place on greased baking sheets. Bake at 350 degrees for 5 to 7 minutes, until dark golden. Cool slightly on pans before removing to wire racks to cool completely. Decorate as desired. Makes 2 dozen.

Vickie

Emily's Gingerbread Cookies

Oatmeal Scotchies

These chewy, delicious cookies are favorites of my family. I used to bake them for my stepson before he went to college...he could almost eat the entire batch by himself!

3/4 c. butter, softened
3/4 c. sugar
3/4 c. brown sugar, packed
2 eggs, beaten
1 t. vanilla extract
1 1/4 c. all-purpose flour
1 t. baking soda
1/2 t. salt
1/2 t. cinnamon
3 c. long-cooking oats, uncooked
11-oz. pkg. butterscotch chips

Beat together butter and sugars until light and fluffy. Add eggs and vanilla; beat well. In a separate bowl, combine flour, baking soda, salt and cinnamon. Gradually add flour mixture to butter mixture, beating until well blended. Stir in remaining ingredients; mix well. Drop by heaping teaspoonfuls 2 inches apart onto ungreased baking sheets. Bake at 375 degrees for 8 to 10 minutes, until golden. Cool slightly on baking sheets; remove to a wire rack to cool completely. Makes 4 dozen.

Abigail Smith
Columbus, OH

Santa's Whiskers

In years gone by, I always made dozens of Christmas cookies to share with family & friends. This recipe is one of my son's favorites…he just loves the maraschino cherries!

1 c. butter, softened
1 c. sugar
2 T. milk
1 t. vanilla extract
2 1/2 c. all-purpose flour
3/4 c. maraschino cherries, drained and finely chopped
1/2 c. pecans, finely chopped
3/4 c. sweetened flaked coconut

Blend together butter and sugar; mix in milk and vanilla. Stir in flour, cherries and pecans. Form dough into 2 logs, each 8 inches long. Roll logs in coconut to coat dough. Wrap in wax paper or plastic wrap; chill dough for several hours to overnight. Slice 1/4-inch thick; place on ungreased baking sheets. Bake at 375 degrees until edges are golden, about 12 minutes. Makes 5 dozen.

Kendra Walker
Hamilton, OH

Georgia Tea Cakes

The perfect "company is coming" goodie! These are so easy to bake up in a jiffy…you probably already have all the ingredients in your kitchen. Yummy with tea or coffee and conversation.

1 c. sugar
1/2 c. butter, softened
1 t. vanilla extract
1 egg, beaten
1/2 c. milk
2 to 2 1/2 c. self-rising flour
Garnish: colored sugar

Mix together sugar, butter, vanilla, egg and milk. Stir in enough flour to make a stiff dough. Drop by teaspoonfuls onto greased baking sheets; sprinkle with colored sugar. Bake at 375 degrees for 9 to 10 minutes. Center should be soft when cooled. Makes about one dozen.

Denise Jones
Fountain, FL

Santa's Whiskers

NOEL

JOY

MERRY CHRISTMAS

105

Winslow Whoopie Pies

Winslow Whoopie Pies

This yummy and often-requested family recipe is a huge hit at any social gathering. I like to tint the filling with food coloring to match the occasion!

$\frac{1}{3}$ c. baking cocoa
1 c. sugar
1 egg, beaten
$\frac{1}{3}$ c. oil
$\frac{3}{4}$ c. milk
2 c. all-purpose flour
1 t. baking soda
$\frac{1}{8}$ t. salt
1 t. vanilla extract
Optional: Christmas sprinkles

In a bowl, combine cocoa and sugar. In another bowl, beat egg and oil; add to cocoa mixture and stir in remaining ingredients except sprinkles. Drop by rounded tablespoonfuls onto lightly greased baking sheets. Bake at 350 degrees for 15 minutes. Let cool. Frost the flat sides of half the cookies with Marshmallow Filling; top with remaining cookies. Roll edges in sprinkles, if using. Makes one dozen.

Marshmallow Filling:

2 c. powdered sugar
$\frac{1}{3}$ c. shortening
$\frac{1}{3}$ c. butter, softened
2 T. milk
6 T. marshmallow creme
1 t. vanilla extract

Combine all ingredients; stir until smooth.

Carissa Ellerd
Thomaston, ME

Blueberry Linzer Tarts

Any flavor of preserves will work in these divine cookies!

1 1/4 c. butter, softened
2/3 c. sugar
1 1/2 c. almonds, ground
1/8 t. cinnamon
2 c. all-purpose flour
6 T. blueberry preserves
powdered sugar

Blend butter and sugar until light and fluffy. Stir in almonds, cinnamon and flour, 1/2 cup at a time. Cover and refrigerate for about one hour. On a lightly floured surface, roll out half of dough 1/8-inch thick. Cut out 24 circles with a 1/2-inch mini cookie cutter; leave remaining 12 circles uncut. Arrange one inch apart on ungreased baking sheets. Bake at 325 degrees for 10 to 12 minutes, until golden. Cool completely on a wire rack. Thinly spread preserves over solid circles; sprinkle cut-out cookies with powdered sugar. Carefully sandwich solid and cut-out cookies together. Spoon a little of remaining jam into cut-outs. Makes one dozen.

Cathy Hillier
Salt Lake City, UT

Add your own special decorating touch to Winslow Whoopie Pies. Pretty little holiday shapes let the preserves peek through, making Blueberry Linzer Tarts a fancy cookie treat.

Blueberry Linzer Tarts

107

our Favorite ITALIAN Recipes

Spice up the holidays with flavors the whole family will love! The delicious aroma of Chicken Piccata or a Deep-Dish Sausage Pizza will bring everyone running to the kitchen to see what you are making. And while these dishes are baking in the oven, you'll have time to visit with the holiday crowd! A beautiful green salad will be a wonderful change of pace from the sweets of the season…serve Panzanella Salad with a favorite soup for a light holiday meal. And Layered Ravioli Florentine is sure to be an asked-for dish every year. So gather up the spices and start cooking Italian for that special Christmas get-together.

Chicken Piccata

Chicken Piccata

As children we always requested our favorite "Flattened Chicken," because Mom used a mallet to pound the chicken flat. She always said it was a good recipe to relieve stress! Cooked angel hair pasta or rice goes very well with this.

12 boneless, skinless chicken
    tenderloins
$^1/_2$ t. pepper
$^1/_2$ t. garlic powder
1 egg, beaten
2 T. milk
1 c. dry bread crumbs
1 T. butter
2 T. oil
$^1/_2$ c. water
$^1/_4$ c. lemon juice
1 t. cornstarch
1 t. chicken bouillon granules
Garnish: chopped fresh parsley
    and lemon wedges

Flatten chicken between 2 layers of plastic wrap with a mallet; sprinkle with pepper and garlic powder. Whisk egg and milk together. Dip chicken in egg mixture; coat with bread crumbs. Melt butter and oil in a skillet over medium heat. Sauté chicken for 4 to 5 minutes on each side, until cooked through. Set aside chicken and keep warm; drain skillet. Whisk together water, juice, cornstarch and bouillon. Add to skillet and simmer until blended; pour over chicken. Serves 6.

*A.M. Gilstrap
Easley, SC*

Herb Focaccia Bread

This crispy, crunchy bread is easy to make and bakes in only 10 minutes.

1 11-oz. tube refrigerated French
    bread dough
2 T. olive oil
1 t. kosher salt
1 t. pepper
1 t. dried oregano
1 t. dried basil
$^1/_2$ t. dried thyme
Optional: marinara sauce, warmed

Unroll dough and pat into an ungreased 15" x10" jelly-roll pan. Press the handle of a wooden spoon into dough, making indentations one inch apart. Drizzle with oil and sprinkle with remaining ingredients except sauce. Bake at 375 degrees for 10 minutes, or until golden. Cut in rectangles and serve with warm marinara sauce for dipping, if desired. Serves 8.

*Irene Robinson
Cincinnati, OH*

Antipasto Kabobs

Easy-to-pick-up party food! Enjoy any time of year by adding some crunchy bread sticks for a light meal during warmer months.

1/3 c. olive oil
1/3 c. balsamic vinegar
1 T. fresh thyme, minced
1 clove garlic, minced
1 t. sugar
9-oz. pkg. refrigerated cheese tortellini, cooked
5-oz. pkg. thinly sliced salami
12-oz. jar artichoke hearts, drained and quartered
5³/4-oz. jar green olives with pimentos, drained
16-oz. jar whole banana peppers, drained
1 pt. cherry tomatoes
16 6-inch skewers
Garnish: fresh basil leaves

Combine oil, vinegar, thyme, garlic and sugar; set aside. Thread remaining ingredients onto skewers alternately in order given. Arrange skewers in a single layer in a glass or plastic container; drizzle with marinade. Cover and refrigerate for 2 to 3 hours, turning occasionally. Drain and discard marinade before serving. Garnish with fresh basil leaves. Makes 16 skewers.

Citrus-Mint Orzo Salad

This recipe is a family favorite from my late mom. It is a much-requested dish for gathering with family & friends.

16-oz. pkg. orzo pasta, uncooked
1 c. olive oil & vinegar salad dressing
1/2 c. frozen orange juice concentrate, thawed
1/2 c. fresh mint, minced
1/2 c. dried apricots, chopped
1 c. currants
1 c. slivered almonds, toasted
1 c. sun-dried tomatoes, chopped
1 green pepper, diced
1 c. red onion, minced
Optional: 1 c. goat cheese, cubed, salt and pepper to taste
Garnish: thin orange slices, fresh mint sprigs

Cook orzo according to package directions; drain and rinse with cold water. Measure out 3 cups cooked orzo into a large serving bowl; reserve remaining orzo for another recipe. In a separate bowl, whisk together salad dressing, orange juice and mint. Drizzle dressing over orzo and mix well. Add remaining ingredients except garnish; toss gently. Garnish as desired. Serves 6 to 8.

JoAlice Welton
Lawrenceville, GA

Antipasto Kabobs

Antipasto Kabobs are such fun to make and eat...make plenty for the whole gang! Perfect for a holiday evening meal, Deep-Dish Sausage Pizza goes together quickly and will please everyone!

Deep-Dish Sausage Pizza

Deep-Dish Sausage Pizza

Why go out to a pizza parlor when you can feast on a hot, hearty pizza right from your own kitchen? It's chock-full of the great Italian sausage and sweet pepper flavors that we love.

16-oz. pkg. frozen bread dough, thawed
1 lb. sweet Italian pork sausage, casings removed
2 1/2 c. shredded mozzarella cheese, divided
1 green pepper, cut into squares
1 red pepper, cut into squares
28-oz. can diced tomatoes, drained
3/4 t. dried oregano
1/2 t. salt
1/4 t. garlic powder
1/2 c. grated Parmesan cheese

Press thawed dough into the bottom and up the sides of a greased 13"x9" baking pan; set aside. In a large skillet, crumble sausage and cook until no longer pink; drain. Sprinkle sausage over dough; top with 2 cups mozzarella cheese. In the same skillet, sauté peppers until slightly tender. Stir in tomatoes and seasonings; spoon over pizza. Sprinkle with Parmesan cheese and remaining 1/2 cup mozzarella cheese. Bake, uncovered, at 350 degrees for 25 to 35 minutes, until crust is golden. Serves 8.

Kathleen Sturm
Corona, CA

Big Eddie's Rigatoni

This recipe was created by my eighty-four-year-old father who has always been a great cook and is affectionately called "Big Eddie" by family members. It's a delicious and satisfying meal when paired with salad and garlic bread.

16-oz. pkg. rigatoni pasta, uncooked
1/8 t. salt
2 lbs. lean ground beef
1 1/2-oz. pkg. spaghetti sauce mix
45-oz. jar chunky tomato, garlic and onion pasta sauce
8 slices mozzarella cheese, divided
8 slices provolone cheese, divided
8-oz. container sour cream
Garnish: grated Parmesan cheese

Cook pasta according to package directions; drain, mix in salt and set aside. Meanwhile, in a large, deep skillet over medium heat, brown ground beef; drain. Stir in spaghetti sauce and pasta sauce; heat through. In a greased 13"x9" baking pan, layer half the pasta, 4 slices mozzarella cheese and 4 slices provolone cheese. Spread entire container of sour cream across top. Layer half of ground beef mixture. Repeat layers, except for sour cream, ending with ground beef mixture. Garnish with Parmesan cheese. Bake, uncovered, at 350 degrees for 30 minutes, or until bubbly. Serves 8.

Mary Beth Laporte
Escanaba, MI

Panzanella Salad

Panzanella Salad

Enjoy this farm-fresh salad any time of year. If you can't find heirloom tomatoes, large red tomatoes will be just as good.

2 lbs. heirloom tomatoes, diced
1/4 c. red onion, minced
2 t. garlic, minced
1/2 c. olive oil
2 T. lemon juice
2 T. fresh basil, chopped
1 T. fresh tarragon, chopped
1 t. salt
pepper to taste
2 c. arugula leaves
Garnish: grated Parmesan cheese

Place tomatoes in a colander to allow liquid to drain; set aside. Combine remaining ingredients except arugula and garnish. Top with Homemade Croutons and toss well. Divide tomato mixture among 4 serving plates. Top each serving with arugula; garnish with cheese. Serves 4.

Homemade Croutons:
1/4 c. butter
1 T. garlic, minced
6 slices day-old bread, crusts trimmed, cubed
salt and pepper to taste
6 T. grated Parmesan cheese

Melt butter in a large skillet over medium heat. Cook until butter foams. Add garlic and cook 30 seconds to one minute. Add bread cubes and toss to coat. Season with salt and pepper. Transfer to a baking sheet and bake at 375 degrees for about 15 minutes, until lightly golden. Sprinkle with cheese and toss until cheese melts. Serves 6 to 8.

Kelly Anderson
Erie, PA

Layered Ravioli Florentine

This delicious, cheesy dish is similar to lasagna, but goes together quickly using frozen ravioli.

10-oz. pkg. frozen chopped
   spinach, thawed and drained
15-oz. container ricotta cheese
1 c. shredded mozzarella cheese,
   divided
1 c. shredded Parmesan cheese,
   divided
1 egg, beaten
1 t. Italian seasoning
16-oz. jar marinara sauce,
   divided
25-oz. pkg. frozen 4-cheese
   ravioli, divided

Combine spinach, ricotta cheese, $^1/_2$ cup mozzarella cheese, $^1/_2$ cup Parmesan cheese, egg and seasoning; set aside. Spread half of sauce in the bottom of a lightly greased 9"x 9" baking pan. Arrange half of frozen ravioli in a single layer on top of sauce. Top with all of spinach mixture and remaining ravioli, sauce and mozzarella cheese. Bake, covered, at 400 degrees for 30 minutes. Remove from oven. Sprinkle with remaining Parmesan cheese; let stand about 15 minutes before serving. Serves 6.

Michelle Campen
Peoria, IL

Layered Ravioli Florentine

Struffoli

Struffoli has been made by our family for generations. Every year between Christmas and New Year's, my children and I spend a day rolling, cutting and frying. The time we spend cooking and talking is priceless.

2 c. all-purpose flour
$^1/_4$ t. salt
3 eggs
1 t. vanilla extract
oil for frying
1 c. honey
1 T. sugar
Optional: sprinkles

In a large bowl, whisk together flour and salt. Add eggs, one at a time, mixing well by hand. Stir in vanilla. Turn dough out onto a lightly floured surface and knead, 5 minutes, until smooth. Divide dough in half and roll out each half to form a $^1/_4$-inch thick rectangle. Cut rectangle into $^1/_4$-inch wide strips and roll each strip into a pencil shape, about 7 inches long. Slice each pencil-shaped roll into $^1/_4$ to $^1/_2$-inch pieces. Add enough oil to a deep skillet to equal 2 inches. Over medium-high heat,

fry several pieces of dough at a time until golden. Drain on paper towels; place in a large bowl. Repeat with remaining dough. In a small skillet over low heat, cook honey and sugar together for 5 minutes. Remove from heat and drizzle over fried pieces; stir gently to coat. Remove from bowl with a slotted spoon; arrange on a large platter. Decorate with sprinkles, if desired. Refrigerate until ready to serve. Serves 12.

Pam Little
Pleasant View, TN

Bright red tomatoes and garden greens combine for a fresh (and holiday-colored!) Panzanella Salad. Serve with plenty of croutons! Hearty and delicious, Layered Ravioli Florentine is just the ticket to warm tummies on a cold night. Serve with fresh bread and a favorite salad.

Project Instructions

Fabric Christmas Cookie Ornaments
(continued from page 10)

1. Trace patterns (page 140) onto tracing paper. For each ornament, use pinking shears to cut 2 pattern pieces from muslin fabric, having wrong sides together and cutting just outside of the outside lines on the pattern. Cut 2 layers of batting, making shapes about ³⁄₈" smaller on all edges than pattern shapes so that batting fits inside the outside running stitch lines.

2. Using washable marking pen, mark stitching lines on fabric front. For ornaments with smaller felted wool pieces, apply to center of fabric with fusible webbing and then embroider and embellish. If adding seed beads, sew on using invisible nylon thread. Sew on buttons, as desired.

3. After fronts are embellished, layer backing fabric, batting hanging loop and decorated front, with wrong sides together. Pin in place. Stitch around outside edges, ¹⁄₈" from outside edges, using 2 strands embroidery floss to make Running Stitches (page 139). Start and stop at the top where the hanger is inserted between fabric layers, stitching over and through hanging ribbon to reinforce loop securely.

Gingerbread House Garland
(continued from page 11)

4. Flatten the paper garland. Cut the small pieces for the doors and windows from the tissue paper. Glue behind the openings in the houses. Let dry.

5. Referring to the lines on the patterns, add details using the fabric paint. Let dry. Glue or tape the finished pieces together as needed to make the length desired.

Felted Holly Trims
(continued from page 12)

4. Coil short lengths (6"-8") of yarn on top of leaves in center to make berries. Handstitch in place by couching over yarn, using matching thread. Sew a length of perle cotton through leaves and knot at ends to make a hanging loop.

Candy Stick Giveaways
(also shown on page 12)

Sweets for the sweet! Candy cane sticks are tied together with string and hung with a paper tag cut from scrapbook paper. Write the message that you wish and glue to the tag for a quick tree trim.

Candy Stick Topper
(also shown on page 12)

Make a topper for your tree in no time! Use hot glue to adhere the candy sticks to a foam wreath form. Then hot glue a favorite vintage ornament to the center of the candy sticks. Wire to the tree.

15 minutes. Remove the apples from the mixture and place on a wire rack and place rack on a baking sheet. Place in a 175 degree oven with the door ajar for about 6 hours. Turn once during the drying process.

2. For oranges, slice the oranges into $^1/_4$" slices. Place on a drying rack and place in a 200 degree oven for about 2 hours. Remove from oven and leave on drying rack to air dry. **Note:** Oranges need only be partially dried. They will finish drying on the wreath.

To make the wreath:
Use floral picks to attach the dried fruit to the wreath where desired. Add berry pokes between fruits. Wrap the wreath with the ribbon and add a ribbon bow.

Friendly Felted Village
(continued from page 15)
Dimensions: $6^1/_2$" h, $3^1/_2$" w

1. Trace full-size patterns (page 142) adding a $^1/_8$" seam allowance when cutting out patterns. All the seaming is stitched close to the edge as the seams remain exposed. Cut from felt. **Note:** Most of the roofs are cut with the heavy felted cable sweater fabric.

2. Stack a gabled side over house side; machine stitch the layers together down the left side. Open the connected pieces and then lay the second gabled side over the other side of the house side and machine stitch the edges together.

3. Lay the second side piece over the open edge of the second gabled piece and machine stitch the edges together. Line up and stitch the right side of the gabled side

to the open edge of the second side piece connecting the 4 walls.

4. Fit the roof over the top of the house structure. Place the edge of the roof under the slanted gable and slide it under the presser foot. Starting at the bottom edge of the gable, machine stitch up one side of the gable, pulling the edge of the roof piece in position as you stitch. When you reach the top, set the needle, lift the presser foot and pivot the fabric.

5. Align the second half of the roof piece under the other half of the gable. Continue your seam until you reach the end of the gable. Repeat the process to attach the other side of the roof to the other gable. Stretch one side of the roof across the top of one of the house sides; if possible pin it in place, and then machine stitch the 2 edges together. Repeat the process and stitch the other side of the roof to the other house side.

6. Working with one side at a time, line up a side of the house base with a gabled/side house piece. Make a single machine stitched seam to connect the base to one side of the house; cut the thread. It's important not to connect the base in a continuous seam, which would bunch and pucker at the corners. Repeat the process to connect 2 more sides to the base. Leave one edge open for stuffing. Knot and trim all the threads. Lightly stuff the house with polyester fiberfill.

7. Cut outer and inner door and window patterns out of felt scraps. The outer windows are $1^1/_2$" square, the inner windows are 1" square, the door is 2" h x $1^1/_2$" w, the door window is $^3/_4$" h x $^1/_2$" w. Pin to the sides of house. Use a full strand of embroidery floss to make a series of small stitches that span from the edges of the outer windows or door to the wall behind it. The inner door and windows are attached by 4 separate $^1/_2$" long stitches, that intersect in the center for a cross shape. Tuck knot under or behind the appliquéd doors and windows.

8. Stitch a button doorknob halfway down one side of the door, knot and trim the thread. Cut a $2^3/_4$" x 3" piece of cardboard base and slide it into the opening at the bottom of the house. Stretch the felt over the edge of the cardboard trapping it inside. If necessary trim the cardboard until it stretches the base but still slides in comfortably. Pin the felt edges together.

9. Carefully insert the pinned edge into the sewing machine and stitch it closed, removing the pins as you stitch.

Fruit-Inspired Luminarias
(continued from page 13)

1. Trace the desired full-size patterns (page 141). For each jar, cut out the shape and tape it in the desired position on the inside of the jar. Use the pattern to paint the fruit shape on the jar, blending white with the color to make a highlighted top. Let the paint dry.

2. Apply the base coat of the crackle mixture to the painted fruit shape as directed by the manufacturer. Follow each of the crackling technique steps as directed, ending with the enhancer to make the appearance of crackling stand out. Let dry. Tie a ribbon bow around jar.

Dressed-Up Wreath
(continued from page 14)

To dry the fruit:

1. For apples, mix together the salt and lemon juice in a small bowl. Wash and dry the apples and slice the apples into $^1/_4$" slices. Use Red Delicious apples sliced from top to bottom for a heart shape. Cut crosswise for circles. Place the the apple slices into the lemon juice mixture until completely covered. Let apples set in the mixture for about

Pillow Ticking Stockings

(continued from page 16)

1. Enlarge and trace patterns (page 143) onto tracing paper and cut out. Cut out stocking, heel, toe and cuff pieces. Fold under $1/2$" on inside curved edges of heel and toe pieces and press. Place heel and toe pieces onto front and back of stocking pieces. Pin in place and baste around outside edges.

For red stocking, use 2 strands off-white embroidery floss to make large running stitches close to edge of stocking heel and toe pieces, going through all layers.

For green stocking, place length of rickrack at inside curved edge of heel and toe pieces and pin in place. Using all 6 strands embroidery floss, loop thread around rickrack from inside point, through toe and stocking body fabric, to inside point of next rickrack section. Go from inside point to inside point, through layers of fabric to attach rickrack to stocking, making the striped effect.

2. Baste batting to back sides of both stocking front and back. With right sides together and using $1/2$" seam, stitch stocking front to back from top edge, around sides and lower edges. Cut red or green fabric into a $2 1/2$" x 8" strip for hanging loop. With right sides together, stitch long sides of loop, using $1/4$" seam. Turn and press. Fold loop in half and place cut edges even with top edge of stocking at side seam, with loop inside stocking.

3. With right sides together and $1/2$" seams, stitch short side seams of cuff and cuff lining pieces, making 2 loops. Stitch cuff lining to cuff, stitching $1/2$" seam at bottom edge. Turn and press.

4. For red stocking, using needle and string sew one length of buttons at a time onto string, knotting string occasionally to keep buttons in place. Insert needle at bottom outside edge of cuff, knotting string inside to secure. String lengths of buttons at about $1 1/4$" intervals across the bottom of the stocking cuff.

5. For green stocking, lay lengths of rickrack across bottom of cuff and pin in place, pinning top row of rickrack about 1" from bottom row. Attach rickrack to cuff, stitching with six strands off-white embroidery floss, looping over rickrack at center of inset part of rickrack. Sew through background fabric. Stitch rickrack to heel and toe sections in the same manner. Put right side of cuff to inside of stocking against fleece. Sew around top edge using $1/2$" seam, sewing through hanging loop. Turn cuff to outside and press at top edge.

6. To make tag, cut one piece of green fabric 4"x6". Trace lettering for name in center of this fabric piece. Using 2 strands embroidery floss, backstitch over lines to make name. Center tag pattern over name and cut out. Lay rickrack along bottom straight edge of tag front and couch on with 6 strands embroidery floss, as with the decorative trim on stocking. Cut one additional tag piece from green fabric and thin batting. With right sides of fabric together and batting on the back, stitch around outside edges in $1/4$" seam allowance, leaving an opening for turning. Clip corners and trim batting from seam line. Turn and press. Slipstitch opening closed. Using 6 strands embroidery floss, stitch button at point of tag and secure it by the stocking hanging loop by taking a few stitches through stocking lining and securing remaining length of thread to the back of the tag.

Quilted Tree Table Runner and Appliquéd Tree Napkin

(continued from page 17)

2. Use $1/4$" seams for all stitching on all pieces. Piece together 5 green and 4 checked $2 1/2$" squares to make a total of four 4-patch blocks. Referring to diagram, below, fuse 3 trees onto each of the $6 1/2$" x $18 1/2$" pieces of green fabric, spacing the shapes evenly across the fabric. Fuse one tree shape onto each of the $6 1/2$" blocks. Stitch around outside edges of tree shapes with hand or machine buttonhole stitches, using darker green thread.

3. Referring to diagram, below, stitch a 4-patch block onto each end of rectangular piece with 3 trees. Stitch $6 1/2$" tree blocks onto each end of $6 1/2$" x $18 1/2$" muslin piece. Stitch all 3 rows together with muslin strip in the middle. Trace small tree shape onto tracing paper and cut out. Lay small tree shape onto muslin section and mark around shape with water soluble marking pen, placing it in random places to mark quilting lines. Layer top, batting and checked backing fabric and baste together. Quilt around tree shapes in center muslin square, filling in between with random pointed stipple lines. Quilt the rest of the table runner, as desired.

4. Appliqué large tree shape onto one corner of napkin. Cut binding strips from striped fabric and sew to outside edges of table runner and napkin, mitering at corners.

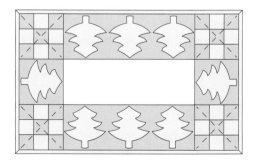

Handy Sewing Tote and Blooming Pincushion

(also shown on page 19)
(Finished size approx. 12" x 12" x 7")

- $5/8$ yard of main color fabric:
  cut two 16" x 20" for body of bag
  cut two $2^1/4$" x 29" for handles
- $5/8$ yard each of contrast fabrics:
  cut two 16" x 20" for inside lining (yellow)
  cut one $2^1/4$" x 42" for lining side binding (yellow)
  cut two $5^1/2$" x $10^1/2$" for front pocket (blue)
  cut one $2^1/4$" x 42" for top binding (blue)
  cut two $7^1/2$" x $8^1/2$" for front pocket (blue)
  cut two $7^1/2$" x $9^1/2$" for handle lining (pink)
- five $3^1/2$" squares assorted fabrics for prairie points
- four $7^1/2$" x $9^1/2$" pieces for inside pockets from contrast print

Additional supplies for bag:

- medium to heavyweight iron-on interfacing:
  cut two 16" x 20" for body of bag
  cut two 7" x 9" for inside pockets
  cut one 5" x10" for outside pocket
  cut one 7" x 8" for outside pocket
  cut four 1" x 28" for handles
- $1/8$" thick upholstery foam (headliner):
  cut two $12^3/8$" x $11^5/8$" for front/back
  cut four $3^1/2$" x $11^5/8$" for sides
  cut one $7^3/8$" x $12^3/8$" for bottom
- $1^1/8$ yard jumbo pink rickrack
- $1/2$ yard $5/8$"w ivory lace
- $1/2$ yard single fold gold bias tape
- 5 assorted buttons
- two 28" lengths of yellow tape measure ribbon
- matching sewing threads

For Pincushion:

- tracing paper
- marking pen
- two 5" squares fabric (pink)
- two 5" squares lightweight interfacing
- 3" square fabric (yellow)
- small amount polyester fiberfill
- 1" square hook and loop tape
- cream-colored embroidery floss

Directions for Sewing Tote:

1. Use $1/4$" seam allowances for all sewing. Fuse interfacing to back of pockets and outside body pieces of fabric. Stitch the 2 body pieces (16" x 20") together along 20" sides; press seam up. Stitch the 2 lining pieces together along the 20" sides. Press seam down. Layer the front and lining pieces together with wrong sides together. With a marking pen, mark horizontal lines parallel to joining seam, $3^3/4$" from the seam. Stitch along the lines through both layers of fabric.

2. With right sides together, stitch pocket lining pieces to each of the 4 pockets (2 inside bag and 2 on outside front of bag), stitching around all sides for the inside lining pockets and leaving an opening for turning. For the outside pockets, stitch around side and lower edges but not the top edge. Clip corners, turn and press. Center lining pockets 5" from the bottom seam of the lining fabric and edge stitch around side and lower edges.

3. Make prairie points from squares of assorted fabrics. See Illustration, below. Arrange points to top edge of shorter front pocket, overlapping, as desired, and baste to top edge. Baste lace over prairie points, having raw edges even. Sew lace to top edge of longer front pocket and stitch on buttons. Stitch gold bias tape to top edges of front pockets. Pin pockets to front of bag, placing them 4" from the bottom joining seam and 4" from side edges of the bag. Edge stitch around side and lower edges of pockets, reinforcing at the top.

4. Insert foam into bottom section of bag. With marking pen, mark vertical lines $3^5/8$" from the sides of the bag body. Mark four 45 degree lines from bottom horizontal lines up toward the outside cut edge of the bag. Stitch on the vertical and diagonal lines drawn. Slide the large foam pieces between the layers for the front and back of the bag.

5. Stitch short handle lining to handle fabric, along the long edge. The strips will be offset $1/2$" at each end. Press seam open. Fuse an interfacing strip close to the stitching line on the wrong side of both the handle fabric and the lining fabric. Pin yellow tape measure ribbon $5/8$" from long side edges over interfacing of handle pieces. Fold raw edges over to meet the raw edge of the seam allowance and press. Fold the handle in half lengthwise and press. Stitch through all layers close to both long edges. Repeat to make a second handle. Fold ends under $1/2$" and press.

6. Place handles at each end of the bag, placing them $6^1/4$" from each side edge and $1^1/2$" from the top cut edge of the bag. Place handles on the inside of the bag and stitch a small rectangle at the ends of the handles through all layers.

7. With right sides of bag together and lining to the outside, prepare to stitch side seams by folding bottom of bag up to the inside of the bag, folding along bottom center seam. The bottom part of the side seam now has 4 layers with the inside pleat. Stitch side seams through all layers. Fold the binding strip for the lining in half lengthwise, wrong sides together and press. Stitch lining binding strip to each side seam, allowing an extra $1/2$" to tuck under at the bottom of the bag. Fold binding around to enclose the seam allowance and stitch in place.

8. Trim the 4 side panels of foam at a 45 degree angle from bottom corner out to fit in the side slots of the bag. Insert the side foam pieces into the bag. Stitch binding strips for top of bag together to make binding long enough to go around the bag top. Fold binding in half lengthwise, wrong sides together and press. Baste rickrack to top edge of bag. Sew binding over rickrack, with top raw edge even with bag raw edge. Flip binding to back and sew in place over stitching line.

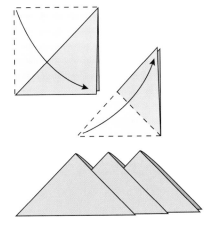

Directions for Pincushion:

(also shown on pages 18, 19)

1. Enlarge and trace patterns (page 144) onto tracing paper and cut out. Fuse interfacing to wrong side of both squares of fabric. On wrong side of one square of fabric, trace around the pattern for the pincushion with marking pen.

2. With right sides together, pin marked square with unmarked square and sew on marked lines. Trim seam allowance to a scant $1/4$", clip corners and curves. Cut a $3/4$" long slit in the center of one layer of fabric. Turn right side out. Stuff lightly with fiberfill and hand stitch opening closed.

3. Use 6 strands embroidery floss to insert needle into pincushion top center. Bring it out at the bottom center, up and around one of the inside points between petals, then through the top center to the bottom.

4. Continue stitching and wrapping embroidery floss between all petals, pulling thread tightly to indent the pincushion. Knot securely.

5. Make yo-yo from smaller square of fabric and sew in center of pincushion. On back of pincushion sew one piece of the hook and loop tape to the center. Sew the other piece of hook and loop tape to the center of the shorter pocket on the front of the bag. Secure pincushion to bag pocket.

Reverse Painting Ornament

(also shown on page 20)

- round flat clear-glass ornament
- pencil
- scissors
- computer-printed letter in reverse to fit ornament center as shown in photograph
- tape
- glass paint, such as Liquitex Glossies, in red, green and white
- small round-tip paintbrush
- $1/2$" flat paintbrush
- 1" w ribbon

1. Carefully wash and dry ornament. Draw a circle $1/4$" outside of letter and cut out on line. Tape letter centered on one side of ornament, printed side down.

2. Using the reversed letter as a pattern, paint the letter red; let dry. Use the small round-tip paintbrush to paint a wreath around the letter using the circle as a guide and small sweeping strokes. Let dry.

3. Add berry dots by dipping the paintbrush handle tip into red paint and dotting randomly around wreath; let dry. Use the flat paintbrush to paint white inside wreath area feathering edges.

4. Let the paint dry. Tie coordinating ribbon bow to the ornament hanger.

Initial Bracelet

(also shown on page 20)

- red and silver beads
- 3 silver charms
- elastic beading thread
- red and silver spacer beads
- round-nose pliers

1. Lay beads and charms in desired order of stringing.

2. String elastic thread with red and silver beads, charms and spacers to fit wrist. Knot ends of each length securely; dot knots with glue.

Dish Towel Apron

(continued from page 21)

1. From one dish towel, cut a piece 16" w by 19" long (for apron center) and 2 pieces $7^{1}/2$" w by $6^{1}/2$" long (for pockets). From other towel, cut 2 pieces $7^{1}/2$" w by 19" long (for side panels). Round the corners of each side panel at lower edge of each side. From the larger calico cut of fabric, cut 2 strips 3" w. Join them in a $1/4$" seam and

cut to a total length of 70". From this same cotton fabric, cut strips 1⅞" w, joining them to make 100" in length.

2. From the coordinating print, cut one strip 1⅞" w to make a length of 30". Feed lengths through bias tape making tool, ironing as strip is pulled through the tool, to make 1" single fold tape.

3. Stitch contrasting print binding to top and bottom edges (7½" length) of pockets. Mark 4" up from the bottom of each side panel and pin pockets to toweling fabric. Stitch through all layers, following binding edge at bottom of pocket and leaving top open for pocket. Baste pocket to side panels at side seams. With wrong sides together, stitch side panels to front of apron along long side edges, using ⅜" seam. Encase the seams with binding. Apply binding to side and lower edges, easing around curves at lower corners.

4. Baste ⅜" in along top edge of apron to gather. Pull up stitches to measure 18". On waistband piece, press ¼" to the back along one long edge. Press ¼" to the back at ends of the waistband strip. Pin band to apron, having the right side of the band to the wrong side of the apron, matching centers. Stitch in ½" seam. Iron ½" to the back on the remaining length of the tie, up to where it joins at the apron edge. Fold waistband in half to the apron front and edge stitch total length of ties and across the apron waist.

Denim Luggage Tags
(also shown on page 21)

- tracing paper
- scraps of denim from discarded denim jeans or shorts
- 3½"x 7" lightweight cotton fabric for each tag backing
- matching sewing thread
- 20" of ⅝" w grosgrain ribbon for each tag
- 4¼"x 3½" piece clear vinyl for each tag

- ¾ yard of ⅛" w decorative trim, if desired
- one grommet set for each tag

1. Trace tag pattern (page 155) onto tracing paper and cut out. For each tag, cut one pattern from denim, centering over small pockets, side seams and other interesting parts of the garment. Cut one from cotton fabric for backing.

2. With wrong sides together, stitch tag front to back, overcasting edges. Use of a heavy jeans needle may be helpful in stitching through multiple denim layers. Place clear vinyl at bottom of tag, matching bottom edges.

3. Straight Stitch (page 139) around side and lower edges of vinyl, stitching through all layers. Stitch decorative trim around outside and lower edges.

4. Apply grommet at center top of tag, according to manufacturer's directions. Fold ribbon in half and pin to top straight edge of tag about 5" down from ribbon fold. Stitch to back of tag.

5. Insert business card or identification slip into the vinyl pocket. To attach to bag handle, pull ribbon ends through grommet hole, wrap loop around handle and insert ribbon ends through loop. Pull ribbon tightly around handle and tie ends together securely.

Embroidered Baby Bib
(continued from page 22)

4. Place band on bib front, 3¼" from bottom edge of bib and pin in place. Attach band to bib by stitching close to pressed edges.

5. For girls' collar, baste lace to outside edges of two collar top pieces, placing lace edge along seam line and extending to the

---

inside of the collar. With right sides together, stitch collar side and lower edges, but not the neckline seam. Clip curves and points, turn and press. Baste collar to right side of bib at neck edge, meeting in center.

6. Place bib pieces right sides together with batting on back of one bib piece. Stitch around all outside edges, leaving an opening for turning. Trim batting close to stitching, clip curves and points, turn and press. Topstitch close to folded edge all around, sewing across open edge used for turning and flipping up collar to sew around neck edge. Stitch in the ditch through all layers on either side of band.

7. Hand sew buttons securely at center front of bib. Stitch hook and loop tape at ends of bib so that rounded edge overlaps on top.

Crochet Toddler Hat
(continued from page 23)

Note: Do not join rnds; but mark beg of each with a safety pin, moving along as you go.

Foundation:

Beginning at the crown with green, ch 2; 3 sc in 2nd ch from hook.

Rnd 2: 2 sc in each sc around – 6 sc.

Rnd 3: Rep Rnd 2 – 12 sc.

Rnd 4: (Sc in next sc, 2 sc in next sc) 6 times – 18 sc.

Rnd 5: (2 sc in next sc, sc in each of next 2 sc) 6 times – 24 sc.

Rnd 6: (Sc in each of next 3 sc, 2 sc in next sc) 6 times – 30 sc.

Rnd 7: (Sc in each of next 2 sc, 2 sc in next sc) 10 times – 40 sc.

Rnd 8: (Sc in each of next 3 sc, 2 sc in next sc) 10 times – 50 sc.

Rnd 9: (Sc in each of next 4 sc, 2 sc in next sc) 10 times – 60 sc.

Rnd 10: (Sc in each of next 5 sc, 2 sc in

(continued on page 120)

next sc) 10 times – 70 sc.

Rnd 11: (Sc in each of next 4 sc, 2 sc in next sc) 14 times – 84 sc.

For size 1: Rnds 12-25: Sc in each sc around. Next Rnd: (Sc2tog) around – 42 sts.

For size 2: Rnds 12-27: Sc in each sc around. Next Rnd: * Sc in next 2 sc, (sc2tog) 20 times; rep from * again – 44 sts.

For size 3: Rnds 12-28: Sc in each sc around. Next Rnd: * Sc in next 4 sc, (sc2tog) 19 times; rep from * again – 46 sts.

Last Rnd (all sizes): * Sl st in each of next 2 sc, in next sc (sl st, ch 2, sl st); rep from * round and fasten off.

Flower

With Plum Wine, ch 4.

Rnd 1: 11 dc in 4th ch from hook; sl st in front lp only of first dc (top of turning ch-3) – 12 dc.

Rnd 2: Working in front lps only of this rnd, (ch 2, 2 dc) in same st as joining, (dc, ch 2, sl st in next st); * sl st, ch 2, 2 dc) in next st, (dc, ch 2, sl st) in next st; rep from * around; do not join – 6 petals.

Rnd 3: Working in rem lps of Rnd 1, sl st in first st; * ch 3, sk next st, sl st in next st; rep from * around, ending ch 3; sl st to beg sl st – 6 ch-3 lps.

Rnd 4: (Sl st, ch 3, 3 tr, ch 3, sl st) in each ch-3 lp around; sl st to beg sl st of Rnd 3.

Rnd 5: * Working in back of petals, ch 4, sl st in next sl st of Rnd 3; rep from * around, ending ch 4; sl st to beg sl st.

Rnd 6: (Sl st, ch 3, 5 tr, ch 3, sl st) in each ch-4 lp around; sl st to beg sl st of Rnd 5. Fasten off.

Join flower to side of hat.

Knit Button-Trimmed Clutch

(continued from page 24)
Gauge: In Garter Stitch (knit every row), 22 stitches = 4"/10 cm.
Take time to check your gauge.

Foundation:

Cast on 44 stitches. Knit every row until piece measures approximately 16" from beginning. Bind off. Weave in loose ends on one side.

Finishing the Bag

1. From cast on edge, fold up 6". Thread a 16" length of cord into yarn needle and sew each side in place. Turn right side out.
2. Baste batting to back of lining. Stitch 1/4" around all outside edges of lining piece. Fold lining to back along stitching lines and press in place.
3. Pin plastic canvas to the back of half the lining and baste seam over the outside and lower edges of the canvas by using matching thread and slip stitching in place.
4. Turn purse inside out. Pin the wrong side of the lining to the wrong side of the purse, having the canvas facing the front of the purse. Using matching thread, hand stitch along lining folded edge, catching in yarn on back side of purse. Turn right side out. Arrange buttons on outside of purse flap and sew in place.
5. Cut ribbon in half. Turn back 1/4" at one end of each ribbon and finger press to form hem. Place a marker on center front of bag 2 1/2" from fold; center hemmed end of one ribbon over marker and sew in place. Fold opposite edge of bag toward first ribbon, find center, sew remaining ribbon to top of flap near the edge. Tie ribbons into a bow.

Easy Fleece Hat and Scarf Set

(also shown on page 24)
- 3/4 yard fleece in desired color
- matching thread
- scissors
- 3 1/2" x 24" piece white fleece (for snowball hat only)

1. Cut off selvages. **For scarf,** cut rectangle with straight or decorative-edge scissors, cutting across the grain of fabric to make a strip 6"x 60". Fold scarf in half and fringe the ends by making 1/2" cuts through both layers, approximately 3" deep. **For hat,** cut a piece of fleece 24" (crosswise grain, with the most stretch) x 8" (lengthwise grain).
2. With right sides together, fold the hat together to make a piece 12"x 8". Stitch back seam, using 1/4" seam allowance, stopping approximately 3" from the edge; backstitch.
3. On bottom edge, fold cuff under 3" to wrong side of hat. Stitch close to cut edge through both layers of fabric. Turn hat right side out and roll up cuff 2 1/2 ". Lay hat flat and fringe top edge by making 1/2" cuts approximately 3" down. Cut strip of fleece 1/2" x 12" long.
4. Gather top of hat together and hold in your hands while using the fleece strip to tie a tight knot around top fringes. Trim strip even with other ties and fluff fringes.

For snowball hat, cut blue fleece 24" (crosswise) x 5 " (lengthwise). Cut white fleece 24" x 3 1/2 ". Connect white fleece to blue fleece by zigzag stitching across the two pieces. Make hat as directed, above, using piece of white fleece to tie top fringes of hat.

Needle Felted Sewing Case
(continued from page 25)

Tools
- needle felting needle
- 3- needle felting tool, such as Clover
- needle felting mat or section of rigid foam insulation
- pinking shears

1. Cut a 6^1/$_4$" x 9^1/$_2$" rectangle out of the 100% white wool felt and the 35% aqua felt. Cut two 9^1/$_2$" long needle strips, one 3" w out of the 35% wool felt pale green, and the other 2" w out of the 100% beige wool felt. Cut two ^{1}/$_2$" x 6" long strips of beige felt for the ties. Use the pattern (page 153) as the guide to cut four leaves out of the pale green.

2. Place the 100% white wool back piece over the needle felting mat. Roll a long strand of brown roving to make a branch. Arrange the branch so that it extends over the bottom edge of the felt. Needle felt the length of the branch in place. Add another small twig section to the branch and needle felt it in place. Create 4 more branches alternating their orientation so they extend off the top and bottom edges of the felt.

3. Highlight some of the branches with strands of pale green roving, needle felting them in place. To make the flower buds, first spiral a strand of beige roving into a circle, needle felt it against the branch.

4. For the petal portion, spiral aqua roving into a circle and needle felt it nestled against the beige. Add one or two more buds to each branch making them smaller as they climb the branch. Highlight the base of each bud with a small strand of light beige, and the petals with a small strand of light aqua.

5. Fold the 100% wool felt beige stem in half and machine stitch the two layers together with a single central stem. Repeat the process with the second strip.

6. Trim the edge of each pair of leaves with pinking shears. Tuck a stem end between the base of two leaves. Pin the leaves together and then center the base of the leaf under the presser foot of the machine. Machine stitch your way up the center of leaf switching directions to make diagonal seams out to the leaf edge and back. Once you reach the top of the leaf, work your way back down filling in with several more diagonal divisions to complete the vein pattern. Repeat the process with the second strip and leaf pair. Trim both edges of the green felt needle strip with pinking shears then center it down the length of the aqua piece. Lay the beige piece down the center of green strip. Pin the strips in place and machine stitch along each edge of the beige strip.

7. Placing right sides together stack the back piece over the inside piece. Place the stems leaf side in between the layers. The stem ends should extend out the edge. Pin the pieces together and then machine stitch around the edges leaving a 2" opening.

8. Turn the piece right side out and hand stitch the opening closed.

9. Hand stitch a single bead to each finished stem, positioning it at the base of a leaf.

Country Pot Holders
(continued from page 26)

to attach and quilt at the same time. Trim around outside edges. Make 1" binding from long strip of cotton fabric. Sew binding around outside edge of block mitering corners. Sew plastic ring or loop of rickrack to one corner for use as hanging potholder.

Cupcake Pincushions
(continued from page 27)

For Smaller Cupcake:
- 8" x 8" square red print fabric
- 8" x 8" square lightweight iron-on interfacing
- 2^1/$_2$" x 7" piece ribbing from recycled sweater
- scrap pink felt for flower embellishment
- scrap red fabric for yo-yo flower
- 8" jumbo pink rickrack
- 22" narrow red cording
- 1" rounded top red button

1. Enlarge and trace patterns (page 146) onto tracing paper and cut out.

2. For Larger Pincushion: Sew short ends of 3" x 11" pink strip together, using ^{1}/$_4$" seam, to form a tube. Cut one large circle for top of cupcake from both the pink fabric and interfacing. Fuse interfacing to back of large circle. Cut appliqué shape for top of large cushion from red felt and appliqué to center of pink circle. Cut yo-yo circle pattern from red print fabric. Make yo-yo and sew button to center. Sew yo-yo to center of appliqué shape. Gather outside edge of pink circle. Pull up basting stitches and pin gathered circle to tube of fabric. Lightly stuff the pink top with polyester fiberfill, adding a small amount of crushed walnuts to the center of the shape and finishing stuffing with polyester fiberfill. Baste around bottom of pink band and pull stitches tight to close shape. Stitch end to reinforce.

3. With right sides together, stitch short ends of ribbing together in ^{1}/$_4$" seam to make a tube. Cut circle for bottom of pincushion from pink felt. Pin ribbing tube to circle and sew in ^{1}/$_4$" seam. Stuff lightly with polyester fiberfill, making a well in the center to add crushed walnut shells for added weight.

(continued on page 122)

4. Insert top into ribbed bottom and pin around top edge of ribbing through top fabric at sewing line where bottom band was added. Hand stitch in place using matching sewing thread. Tack rickrack to the top edge of the sweater fabric, using hand stitches and matching sewing thread.

5. For Smaller Pincushion: Make in same fashion as the larger one. Iron interfacing to the same size circle for the top. Pin cording in coil pattern, radiating from the center of the circle. Couch (page 138) using matching sewing thread. Sew rounded button to center. Baste ³/₄" from outside edge of circle to gather.

6. Pull up threads to draw in fabric to the size of the ribbing tube used as the base. After stuffing top, sew bottom closed. Insert top into sweater ribbing bottom and hand stitch in place. Hand stitch decorative rickrack at the center of the bottom ribbing.

7. Make yo-yo from red fabric and after securing stitching in center of the gathered circle, loop thread over outside of yo-yo and into the center to pull in sections to make petals. Cut small flower shape from pink felt. Sew yo-yo flower to center of pink flower shape, stitch button in center and hand stitch to side of ribbing bottom.

Soft Felted Nests
(continued from page 30)
sweater felt together. Place a branch strip over the connection and stitch it in place to conceal the connection.

4. Using a needle and thread, stitch 3 separate leaf groupings around edge of nest. Stitch some leaves to the branch ends. Place the small flower over the center of the large flower and stitch it in the middle of one of the leaf groupings.

5. Condition the clay in your fingertips until it is pliable. Beige and white clay will form the base of the eggs. Add small pieces of light green or aqua to tint the eggs. Don't fully integrate the 2 colors. The goal is to have the darker color flecked or slightly marbled into the white. Roll the blended clay into three ³/₄" egg shapes. Follow the package directions to harden the clay in the oven. The eggs will rest in the concave center of the nest.

Doe-A-Deer Stocking
Crochet abbreviations are on page 139.
(continued from page 31)

Rows 4-23: Cont working the chart.
Row 24 (WS): With garnet, sc in each sc across; fasten off.

Heel
Row 1: With RS facing, join garnet in 10th sc of back edge (side without deer), ch 1, sc in same sc and next 9 sc, sc in first 10 sc of next side – 20 sts; turn.
Row 2: Ch 1, sc in first 13 sts, leaving remaining sts unworked; turn.
Row 3: Ch 1, sc in first 6 sts, leaving remaining sts unworked; turn.
Row 4: Ch 1, sc in 6 sc, sc in next unworked sc on Row 1; turn.
Row 5: Ch 1, sc in 7 sc, sc in next unworked sc on Row 2; turn.
Rows 6-17: Adding 1 additional st per row, rep Rows 4 and 5 alternately. At end of last row, fasten off. (20 sts)

Foot
Skip first 10 sts of last row on Heel; join garnet in next sc, ch 1, sc in same sc and next 9 sc, skip 3 unworked sts on Stocking Body, sc in next 22 sts, skip last 3 sts on Stocking Body, sc 10 sc of Heel; join with a sl st in first sc – 42 sts; turn.
Rnds 2-20: Ch 1, sc in each sc around, join; turn.

Toe
Rnd 1: Ch 1, (sc in 5 sc, sc2tog) 6 times – 36 sts; join and turn.
Rnd 2 and following evenly numbered rows: Ch 1, sc in each sc around; join and turn.
Rnd 3: Ch 1, (sc in 4 sc, sc2tog) 6 times – 30 sts; join and turn.
Rnd 5: Ch 1, (sc in 3 sc, sc2tog) 6 times – 24 sts; join and turn.
Rnd 7: Ch 1, (sc in 4 sc, sc2tog) 4 times – 20 sts; join and turn.
Rnd 9: Ch 1, (sc in 3 sc, sc2tog) 4 times – 16 sts; join and turn.
Rnd 11: Ch 1, (sc in 2 sc, sc2tog) 4 times – 12 sts; join. Leaving a long tail, cut yarn. Thread tail into yarn needle and weave back through remaining sts; pull up to close opening and secure in place.

Weave in loose ends along WS of stocking. Using garnet, join back seam and small openings on each side of Heel.

Cuff
With WS facing, join green in first remaining ch of Foundation, ch 1, sc in same ch and next 2 ch, changing to bone in last st. (3 bone sc, 3 green sc) around, ending 3 bone sc; join. Ch 1, (3 bone sc, 3 green sc) around, ending 3 bone sc and change to green in last st; join. With green, ch 1, (3 green sc, 3 bone sc) around, ending 3 green sc. Work another rnd as est. Alternate the 4 rows of colored squares 4 times more. Leaving a tail to weave in later, cut bone. With green, ch 1, sc in each sc around; join. Working from left to right for reverse sc, sc in each sc around; join and fasten off.

Hanging Loops
Fold cuff in half to RS of stocking. Holding one strand each of green and bone, join to WS of cuff over the seamed side. (Ch 15, sl st in join) 3 times. Leaving a 10" tail, cut yarn. Wind the double strand around the 3 loops several times then secure in place on WS of cuff.

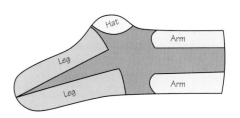

mashed potatoes (about 10-15 minutes). Carefully place clay onto a large piece of foil and cover with a damp cloth. Allow to cool. Keep in plastic bag until ready to use.

Cranberry Ice Globes
(also shown on page 34)
- round balloons
- birdseed, orange peel
- dried cranberries or other dried fruit
- funnel (optional)
- water; freezer

1. Drop the birdseed, dried fruit and orange peel into the empty balloon. (Use a funnel if necessary.) Fill the balloon with water and tie a knot at the top.
2. Place in the freezer turning the balloon every 20 minutes until frozen. Remove from freezer and peel off balloon. Set outside in cold weather for the birds.

Salt Clay Snowflakes
(continued from page 38)
5. Use the markers to make shapes and doodles on the dry clay shapes. Thread a narrow ribbon through the hole for hanging.

Cornstarch Clay
Stir together 2 cups baking soda and one cup cornstarch in a medium saucepan. Slowly add 1 1/4 cups cold water. Stir until dissolved. Cook over medium heat stirring constantly until the mixture looks like

Sweet Sister Dolls
(also shown on page 38)
- one pair of white, finely-woven cotton or cotton blend socks for **each** doll
- tea bags, if dying is preferred (optional)
- tracing paper
- pencil
- 14 1/2" square of blanket fabric and soft lining fabric (for baby doll)
- 2 1/4" buttons for eyes for each doll
- pink embroidery floss
- red colored pencil
- white quilting thread
- 3/4 yard small print fabric (for toddler dress)
- two 2" x 5" strips pink gingham fabric (for toddler dress sleeve ruffles)
- one 2" x 22" strip pink gingham fabric (for toddler dress skirt)
- polyester fiberfill
- yellow curly yarn for hair
- small red button (for toddler doll's dress)
- black crafts paint
- 8" of 1/4" w black satin ribbon (for toddler doll shoes)
- 16" of 1" w satin ribbon (for toddler's skirt)
- 16" of 1" w ribbon (for baby's blanket)
- scrap of cotton (for bloomers)

1. Tea dye sock if desired to obtain a softer color. Let dry. Referring to the diagram, above right, cut sock as shown for the arms and legs for the toddler doll. For the baby doll body, trace pattern (page 148). Lay sock on pattern and cut with toe of sock at top of pattern. Mark all pattern line indications using a pencil.

2. Trace clothing patterns (page 148) onto tracing paper and cut out. Draw around clothing pattern pieces on fabric and cut out. Cut a 9" x 22" piece from small print fabric for toddler skirt. Set aside.
3. To make the bodies, stitch with right sides together using a 1/4" seam. Turn. Stuff body firmly but do not stretch sock.
4. Whipstitch the bottom of the sock closed using quilting thread. **For the toddler,** sew straight across. **For the baby,** follow stitching line on pattern.
5. Move the batting around until the desired face shape is achieved. Using the quilting thread, sew a running stitch on the pencil line. Pull slightly, secure and make a knot. Make 2 pencil dots for the eyes.
6. Using the quilting thread, sew the 2 buttons in place, pulling the thread slightly and knot thread. For the nose, stitch 2 short stitches about 1/8" apart; sew a tiny stitch at the bottom of the stitches, forming a U shape. Pull thread to make nose using tip of needle to pull and shape nose.
7. For the mouth, sew a straight line of pink embroidery thread. With the needle tip, pull the top lip over the thread and pull tight then pull out the bottom lip to make a smile. Color cheeks, tip of nose and bottom lip with a red colored pencil.
8. Cut the heel end of the sock for the hat. Using a sewing machine, pull the edge taut as you are sewing and zigzag the edge with coordinating thread to match the blanket or dress, for a ruffled edge.
9. **For toddler's hair,** cut ten 12" lengths of golden yellow yarn and 12" of 1/4" w pink satin ribbon. Align lengths of yarn and mark center. Pin to center of forehead. Hand stitch down center line, stitching through head to attach. Tack at sides where ears would be by stitching through yarns and stuffed head. Cut ribbon in half and tie where hair is attached to sides of head.

(continued on page 124)

10. For baby's hair, cut five 2¹⁄₂" lengths golden yellow yarn. Coil lengths of yarn at top of head to make curls. Couch (page 138) onto stuffed head using matching sewing thread.

11. Pull hats tightly over dolls heads and fasten using small stitches.

12. For baby doll, sew the front and back pieces of the blanket with right sides together leaving about 3" open. Turn with right sides out and press seams. Top stitch edges of blanket, turning in edges of opening and stitch closed. Fold blanket over baby doll body and tie with satin ribbon.

13. For the toddler doll body, stuff arms and legs firmly using polyester fiberfill and whip stitch arms to body of doll. For the legs, paint shoes using the black crafts paint. When dry, cut black ribbon in half and sew on each side of foot. Tie in bows and trim ends. Sew legs to body of doll.

For bodice top, sew edge of collar under. With right sides of fabric together, sew under arm seam. Turn right side out. For sleeve ruffles, stitch short ends together in ¹⁄₄" seam. Fold lengths in half with wrong sides together. Baste ¹⁄₄" along long unfinished edge to gather. Pin underneath sleeve edge and stitch along stitching line to attach to sleeve. Sew button to bodice front. Put bodice on doll and overlap at back. Stitch to doll body.

For skirt, narrow hem side and bottom edges of skirt. Gather top to fit waist of doll. Center and sew white satin ribbon over gathers. Make skirt ruffle by narrowly hemming sides and lower edge of gingham strip. Baste ¹⁄₄" along long unfinished edge to gather. Stitch ruffle to top of skirt along lower edge of white ribbon. Stitch pink satin ribbon over unfinished edge of ruffle at waist, folding in ends of pink ribbon at sides.

For bloomers, stitch raw edges of hem. With right sides together, sew crotch seam. Turn under small hem on waist and sew a running stitch with quilting thread. Put bloomers on doll. Gather and pull the stitch tight; knot. Put the skirt over the shirt and bloomers and tie in back.

Note: Dolls have small parts and are not intended for children under 3 years old.

Child's Art Wraps
(also shown on pages 38 and 40)
- white craft paper
- crayons or markers
- ribbons to coordinate with crayon colors
- scissors
- clear tape

1. Unroll the craft paper and lay out on a flat surface. Have the children draw and color on the white paper using crayons and markers.

2. Lay package to be wrapped on the paper. Cut enough to wrap the package. Secure with tape. Add desired ribbon.

Paper Doll Dress Trims
(continued from page 39)

4. Using a flat paintbrush or even a straight side of poster board, make sure the glue is applied in a thin layer. Lay fabric clothing onto the poster board clothing and press firmly making sure there are no bubbles under the fabric. When the glue is no longer tacky, glue on the decorative pieces, collars, cuffs, sailor skirt, mittens, ribbons, rickrack or front dress facing. For the buttons, sew thread into button holes with thread and glue on buttons.

5. When all desired fabric trims are applied, turn clothing over and trim any excess fabric with scissors. Using transfer paper, copy lines of fabric folds onto fabric and then trace over lines with the black permanent marker. Add ribbon or floss for hanging.

Bandanna Art Trim
(continued from page 40)

1. Cut the bandanna in half making 2 triangles. Referring to diagram 1, below, fold up long bottom edge along fold line. Turn over. Referring to diagram 2, below, fold along outside dotted line. Referring to diagram 3, below, fold on inside dotted line. Whip stitch where the two sides meet. Use paint pen to make dots or other designs on the bandanna. Let dry.

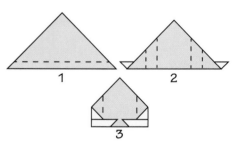

2. Fold tissue paper to fit opening and fill with cookies or candy. Use a needle threaded with floss to make a hanger for the Trim.

Sweet Candy Ornament

(also shown on page 40)
- 6 hard candies, such as Life Savers in desired colors
- baking sheet
- aluminum foil
- oven
- string

1. Arrange 5 candies in a circle with one on top on an aluminum foil-lined baking sheet. Be sure all of the candies are touching.
2. Bake at 250 degrees for about 5 minutes until candies have just started to melt together. Watch carefully because oven temperatures vary. Remove from oven and let cool on baking sheet.
3. Remove from sheet and thread the string through the top hole for hanging.

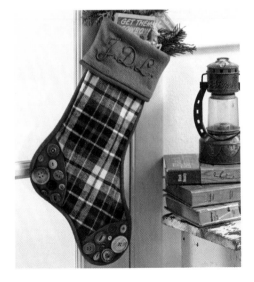

Monogram Wool Stocking

(continued from page 46)
2. Apply interfacing to wrong sides of plaid stocking pieces. On red heel and toe pieces, turn under inside curved edges ¹/₄" and

press. Pin to plaid stocking front and stitch close to folded edges of heel and toe pieces. Baste outside edges to stocking. Arrange the buttons on the heel and toe pieces and stitch in place.
3. Wrap long strips of red wool fabric around cording and baste close to cording. Stitch cording around stocking front, with raw edges even and using a ¹/₄" seam. With right sides together, stitch stocking front to stocking back, using ¹/₄" seam. Clip curves, turn right side out and press. With right sides together stitch red lining pieces together using ¹/₄" seam. Clip curves. Slip lining inside plaid stocking, with lining wrong side facing stocking wrong side. Baste around top edges.
4. Print out letters to be used for monogram. On right side of one gray cuff piece, center letters to be used. Slide carbon paper underneath letters and trace letters onto cuff front. Pin red cording over traced lines and Couch on cording using matching sewing thread. With right sides together, stitch cuff front to cuff back at side seams using ¹/₄" seam. Repeat for cuff lining. On cuff front, stitch red piping to lower edge, stitching close to cording. With right sides together, stitch cuff to cuff lining at lower edge, using ¹/₄" seam. Turn and press. Baste top edges together.
5. For hanging loop, fold strip of red fabric in half and stitch down long side in ¹/₄" seam. Turn right side out and press. Fold loop in half and place raw edges of loop at side edge of stocking, having loop extend down toward center of stocking. Pin at top side edge. Place cuff inside stocking, with right side of cuff next to the right side of the red stocking lining fabric, with monogrammed lettering to the front button edge of stocking. Pin in place and stitch around top edge in ¹/₂" seam allowance. Edge stitch close to seam line on lining fabric. Flip cuff over to outside of stocking and press.

Crochet Poinsettia Blossom

(also shown on page 47)
Skill Level: Easy
Size: About 7" wide

- Caron Simply Soft, 100% acrylic yarn, (6oz/170g/315yd/288m) per skein: One skein of Red #9729
- size E/4 (3.5mm) crochet hook or size needed to obtain gauge
- six ¹/₄" diameter dark yellow buttons
- black sewing thread

Gauge: First leaf measures 3" long and 2" across widest portion.
Take time to check your gauge.

Foundation:
Ch 5; join with sl st in first ch to form a ring.

Leaf
1. Leaving a 10" tail, ch 15. Sc in 2nd ch from hook; * working 1 st into each ch work 1 hdc, 3 dc, 4 tr, 3 dc, 1 hdc **, 1 sc. Working 1 st into each ch along opposite edge, sc in first ch then rep from * to ** again, 3 sc in last ch. Sc in each of 29 sts, 2 sc in next st. Sl st in 15 sc then sl st in ring.
2. Make 4 more leaves as est. After 5th leaf, leave a 10" tail, fasten off. Take tails to WS and tie into an overhand knot.

Finishing
Sew tiny buttons to center of flower using black thread. Tie off ends.

Bias Tape Birdie Set
(continued from page 48)

of tape at bottom ends for tail. Pin in place and stitch with small hand stitches. Curve top pieces of bias tape over bottom pieces for bird bodies, tucking under both cut ends. Pin in place and stitch.

3. Using 3 strands black embroidery floss, make French Knots (page 138) for eyes and Stem Stitch (page 139) to make feet. Using 3 strands gold embroidery floss, make Stem Stitch in small triangular shapes for beaks.

Potholder
- one white dish towel (approximately 18" x 27")
- 10" lengths each of red extra wide double fold bias tape, blue and green single fold bias tapes
- 9" blue double fold bias tape
- gold embroidery floss
- matching sewing threads
- marking pencil
- 10" x 26" piece of heat-resistant batting

1. From towel, cut two 10" squares. Cut two 6" x 10" pieces, having both pieces with one 10" side using hemmed edge of towel. From batting, cut one 10" square and two 6" x 10" pieces.

2. On one 6" x 10" piece of toweling, place red bias tape $1/2$" from hemmed long side. Pin and stitch in place using matching sewing thread. Place blue tape $1/4$" from edge of red tape and sew in place using matching sewing thread. Place green tape $1/4$" from edge of blue tape and sew in place using matching sewing thread. Make French Knots using 3 strands gold embroidery thread. Layer the remaining 6"x10" piece of toweling, 6"x10" piece of batting and decorated piece

of 6"x10" toweling, having towel hemmed edges together for pocket top. Baste around outside edges and stitch close to hemmed edges through all layers.

3. Place batting on back of both 10" toweling squares. With marking pencil, mark stitching lines to quilt layers together. Stitch through toweling and batting. Sew close to side edge of blue bias tape using matching sewing thread. Fold loop in half and place at top right corner of one 10" toweling square, having raw edges even at corner and loop hanging to inside of square. Place pocket over this same square, aligning bottom edges. Baste around outside edges.

4. With right sides together, pin potholder front to back. Stitch around outside edges in a $1/2$" seam, leaving an opening for turning. Trim batting close to seam line and clip corners. Turn right side out and sew opening closed with matching sewing thread.

Mother/Daughter Country Aprons
(continued from page 50)

- Cut 3 blocks $8 1/4$" square. Subcut diagonally twice for 12 quarter square triangles (QST's). You will need 10 of the QST's. Enlarge pattern (page 144) and cut 2 pockets.
- From green fabric cut one piece 4" x $36 1/2$".
- From stripe fabric cut one piece $1 1/2$" x $36 1/2$".

Daughter's apron:
- From yellow fabric cut one piece $20 1/2$" x $8 1/2$".
- From red fabric cut waist band $3 1/2$" x 44". Enlarge flap pattern (page 144) and cut 8 flaps. Enlarge pocket pattern (page 144) and cut 4 pockets.
- From green fabric cut one piece 3"x $20 1/2$".
- From stripe fabric cut one piece $1 1/4$" x $20 1/2$".

1. Use $1/4$" seam allowance, unless otherwise instructed, with right sides together. Press seams as you sew.

2. Sew the stripe piece to a long edge of the yellow piece. **For mother's apron,** sew 2 red QST's together, sewing on the diagonal edges. Make 5. Trim points and turn right side out. **For daughter's apron,** sew 2 flaps together, sewing on the curved edge. Make 4. Turn right side out and press.

3. Pin the raw edges of the flaps or QST's to the edge of the stripe piece, aligning raw edges and starting $1/2$" from the side edge. Space evenly up to $1/2$" from the opposite side edge. Overlap the QST units by $1/4$". Pin the green piece on top of the flaps or QST's, right sides together and aligning all edges. Sew together. Fold a double $1/4$" hem on the side and bottom edges and sew.

4. Sew 2 pocket pieces together, sewing on all sides and leaving a 1" opening. Trim points and curved edges and turn right side out, press and slip stitch the opening closed. Make one pocket **for the mother's apron** and 2 **for the daughter's apron.**

5. Arrange pockets. **For the mother's apron,** arrange pocket $4 1/2$" from the top edge and 4" from the side edge. **For the daughter's apron,** arrange the pockets $3 1/2$" from the top and side edges. Sew to apron on the side and bottom edges.

6. Sew a gathering stitch across the top of the apron. Draw gathers to $20 1/2$" **for the mother's apron** and 13" **for the daughter's apron.** Space gathers evenly and top stitch across gathers to secure.

7. Determine the center of the apron top and mark with a pin. Determine the center of the waist band lengthwise and mark with a pin. Pin the waist band to the apron top, right sides together and matching the center marks. Sew together.

8. Fold the waist band ends in half lengthwise, right sides together, and pin edges. Sew edges and across each end (do not sew the band behind the apron). Turn right side out and press. Fold $1/4$" hem under on the open area of the waist band and press. Pin to the back of the apron enclosing the seam.

9. Top stitch the band $1/8$" from the edge, sewing all the way around and securing the band to the back of the apron.

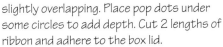

slightly overlapping. Place pop dots under some circles to add depth. Cut 2 lengths of ribbon and adhere to the box lid.

3. To make bow, layer several cupcake liners, alternating directions. Staple in the center, fold in half at the staple and cut slits along the edges to create "petals." Round each with scissors. Unfold and "fluff." Cut one liner a bit smaller for the center of the bow and adhere. Punch a circle for the center and adhere. Knot a short length of ribbon and adhere to the bow, then adhere the bow to the box.

Patchwork Calico Pillows
(continued from page 51)

3. With right sides together, stitch the pillow top to the backing fabric, leaving a 6" opening to insert the pillow form or to stuff. Trim corners; turn right side out.

4. Insert pillow form or stuff pillow, as desired. Stitch opening closed using matching thread and invisible hand stitches.

For red pillow: Sew buttons to front and back, using long needle and upholstery thread. Pull thread tight to gather in at center where buttons are placed.

Toy Topper
(also shown on page 54)

- cardboard box
- 3 colors of coordinating cardstock
- rickrack to fit around box lid
- border punch or strip
- wooden toys
- circle punches in 2 sizes
- twine
- tape adhesive
- hot-glue gun and glue sticks
- marker
- stamps, rub-on letters or computer/ printer (for tag text)

1. Cover box with cardstock using strong tape adhesive. Cover lid with same color and layer with 2 mats of coordinating cardstock. Adhere border made of coordinating cardstock around edges of lid. Adhere rickrack to border. Arrange wooden toys and adhere to lid with hot glue.

2. For tag, string twine through a large circular wooden toy, leaving length to tie. Create text for tag, punch into circle shape, mat onto larger circle, add pen-stitching with marker, then adhere to wooden toy. Tie tag to wooden toys on lid.

Jingle Bell Topper
(also shown on page 54)

- cardboard box
- 3 colors of coordinating cardstock
- one patterned paper
- one large package of glittered jingle bells
- sheer ribbon for bow
- border punch or strip
- small tag
- twine
- tape adhesive
- hot-glue gun and glue sticks
- stamps, rub-on letters or computer/ printer (for tag text)

1. Cover box with cardstock using strong tape adhesive. Cover lid with same color and layer with mats of coordinating cardstock.

2. Adhere patterned paper around the edge of lid. Adhere border made of coordinating cardstock to bottom edge of lid. Adhere bells to lid with hot glue. Tie ribbon into a bow and adhere with hot glue next to bells.

3. Create tag and tie to package with twine.

Cupcake Liner Topper and Box
(continued from page 54)

Outside of box:

1. Cover box and lid in cardstock using tape adhesive.

2. Cut a large mat of coordinating paper for the lid. Cut strips of matching cardstock/ paper and adhere to the edges of the box lid. Punch circles of various sizes from matching cardstock/patterned paper. Punch smaller holes in some of the larger circles to add interest. Adhere circles to sides of box,

Buttons and Bows Topper

(also shown on pages 52 and 55)
- cardboard box
- 4 colors coordinating cardstock
- dotted paper
- scalloped/circle die cuts for top of box
- border punch or strip
- ribbon to wrap around box
- buttons in graduated sizes
- liquid glue
- adhesive foam dots
- tape adhesive

1. Cover box and lid with cardstock using strong tape adhesive. Cover sides of lid in dot paper. Adhere border made from coordinating cardstock to lower edge of lid.
2. Wrap ribbon round sides of box and tape to top of lid. Cut scallop and circle from cardstock and adhere to lid using adhesive foam dots. Arrange buttons as desired, stacking some, and adhere using liquid glue.

Christmas Carol Topper

(also shown on page 55)
- cardboard box
- 3 colors coordinating cardstock
- patterned paper
- old Christmas sheet music
- large scallop and circle die cut

- tag
- twine
- stapler
- hot-glue gun and glue sticks
- tape adhesive
- stamps, rub-on letters or computer/ printer (for tag text)

1. Cover box and lid with cardstock using strong tape adhesive. Cut mat from patterned paper and adhere to lid. Cut large circle and scalloped circle from cardstock and adhere to patterned paper on lid.
2. To make bow, cut 1" strips of sheet music and cardstock—two 9" long, two 8" long and two 7" long. Fold them into loops and staple at the center. Crisscross the two longest strips and use hot glue to secure. Do the same with the next two layers. Add additional layers as desired. Add loops of paper/cardstock to center. Cut "tails" from sheet music and cardstock and hot glue to box as desired. Make tag and trim with patterned paper and cardstock. Tie to package with twine.

Dressed-Up Doggy Cards

(also shown on page 56)
1. To make the card base, fold the full sheet of cardstock in half lengthwise and then cut it in half widthwise (with the paper trimmer). This will divide the paper into two card blanks. The poodle card uses the natural colored card base, and the Dachshund uses the white card base.
2. Ink the snowflake stamp with the aqua stamp pad and randomly stamp the front of the natural card for the poodle card, and the patterned paper for the Dachshund. Ink the message stamp with the black stamp pad and print it on the inside of the card.
3. Carefully rip a 1" tall strip of white paper to make the snow bank for the poodle card. Repeat the process to tear a stamped

patterned paper for the Dachshund card. Trim the sides of the ripped strip to fit across the bottom of the card. Glue the strip in place.
4. Trace the dog and dog clothing patterns (page 154) and cut out. Cut the poodle shapes out of the tan paper and the Dachshund dog shapes out of brown cardstock scraps. Position the dogs on the center front of each card so that their feet stand over the paper snow. Glue each earpiece to the head so the outside edge of the ear extends beyond the head.
5. Cut the collar piece out of the patterned paper and the main coat out of the aqua felt. Cut the single Dachshund coat template out of the red felt.
6. Using red embroidery thread, make a single stitch in and out the center top of the blue felt coat, tie the ends into a bow and then trim the thread ends. Using off-white thread, make a series of small stitches that encircle the collar of the red felt coat. Knot the ends on the wrong side of the felt; trim the ends.
7. Glue patterned collar over base of poodle's neck. Use a thin layer of craft glue to mount the blue felt coat over the poodle's body and bottom edge of collar. Use more craft glue to attach the red coat to the Dachshund. Use a thin permanent marker to add a single eye and an oval nose to each dog.

Fabric-Backed Cards

(also shown on page 56)
For the Tree and Star Cards:
- small piece of small-print fabric
- 4-5 colors of cardstock
- one patterned paper
- Christmas tree punch
- small buttons
- star punch
- twine
- paper piercer
- small punched star
- corner rounder

- small hole punch
- computer or stamp for text
- adhesive, including strong tape, glue pen

1. Cut card base from cardstock, then score and fold in half so that card opens at bottom. Stamp or print text strip and adhere across bottom portion of card.
2. Cut desired shape from cardstock, then cut into shape to fit space above text. Cut fabric and tape to the back of cardstock to show through opening. Mat in slightly larger coordinating cardstock and adhere to card. **For star card,** cut small squares of cardstock to fit in space at right. Add small buttons tied with twine on star card and on trees on tree card. Print or stamp greeting and adhere to inside of card.

Woodland Wrap
(continued from page 57)
1. Cut curved strips of "snow" from white cardstock. Adhere around base of box. Cut triangle "trees" from three shades of green cardstock. Cut small trunks from brown cardstock. Adhere the trees to the box sides as desired, using pop dots under some of them. Adhere snowflakes to box sides as desired.
2. Cut 2 strips of cardstock to create ribbon strips for lid. Trim the ends at an angle, then adhere to lid using strong tape adhesive.
3. To make bow, cut six 1" strips of white cardstock–two 9" long, two 8" long, two 7" long. Fold them into loops and staple at the center. Crisscross the two longest ribbons and use hot glue to secure. Do the same with the next 2 layers. Punch a circle from cardstock and adhere to the center of the bow (to cover staple). Hot glue a pine cone to the center of the bow.

Stamped Paper Bag
(also shown on page 57)
- brown handle bag
- patterned paper
- decorative edge paper
- green and red cardstock
- small holiday stamp and ink
- small tag or tag die
- small circle punch
- floral wire
- pencil
- twine
- needle and floss
- glitter glue
- stamps, rub-on letters or computer/printer (for tag text)

1. Ink edges of bag, then stamp front of bag and color the images with markers. Add glitter to stamped images and allow to dry.
2. For bag topper, cut patterned paper into a square to fit the width of the bag (ours is 8"x 8") and fold in half. Cut a slit in the top for the bag handle. Cut a decorative edge along the bottom of each side. Ink the bag topper, then hand-stitch along edges.
3. Cut holly leaves from green cardstock; punch berries from red. Lightly fold the leaves for dimension. Adhere to bag topper. Coil floral wire around a pencil and wrap around one side of handle.
4. Create tag from coordinating materials; trim with twine and tie to handle with floss.

Torn Paper Wrap
(also shown on page 57)
- cardboard box
- white and coordinating cardstock (to match ribbon)
- brown kraft paper
- wide ribbon to wrap around box and tie
- snowflake die cuts or punches
- glitter glue
- tape adhesive
- adhesive dimensional dots
- manila shipping tag
- computer/printer or stamps for tag text
- needle and floss

1. Cover box and lid in white cardstock using tape adhesive. Cut and adhere a kraft paper mat to box lid. Cut a strip of kraft paper to fit around the edge of the lid.
2. Tear a strip of kraft paper to extend around the box. **Tip:** Tear toward your body slowly to create a rough edge. Tape to box. Tie ribbon around box and knot at top. Tie bow. Adhere glittered snowflakes to top of box using adhesive dimensional dots.
3. **For tag,** adhere white cardstock to base of manila tag. Tear kraft paper and adhere above it. Adhere ribbon to tag for color. Stamp or print text onto matching cardstock; adhere to tag at an angle. Hand-stitch along the bottom of tag using white floss. Adhere glittered snowflake to tag using adhesive dots. Tie tag to lid.

- twine
- adhesive, including glue dots and foam dots
- corner rounder
- ink for edging papers
- computer or stamps for creating inside greeting
- $^1/_8$" and $^1/_2$" circle punches
- scalloped circle die or punch
- paper piercer

1. Cut card base from cardstock. Score and fold so that card opens at right side. Round corners and ink. Cut wide strip of patterned paper, ink and adhere to bottom portion of card. Cut strip of patterned paper for left portion of card. Using a $^1/_2$" circle punch, notch the bottom two corners of the strip, then ink and adhere vertically to left portion of card. Cut a narrower strip of patterned paper, then ink and adhere vertically on top of wider strip.
2. Cut a small tag from contrasting cardstock to mat small rectangular sticker. Punch a hole in the end and string with twine. Ink and set aside.
3. Cut a strip of cardstock to fit width of card. Knot wide ribbon around the left portion of this strip. Before completing knot, tie twine to the ribbon, then complete the knot. Trim ribbon then adhere strip to card. Mat round image onto a scalloped circle cut from cardstock. Use a piercing tool to make small holes in each of the scallops. Ink and then position the scalloped piece at the middle right of the card, extending off edge. Trim flush with right edge. Adhere the sticker to the center of the scallop using foam pop dots. Print or stamp greeting; adhere to inside of card.

Warm Wishes Snowman Card
(continued from page 58)
5. Adhere narrow ribbon along bottom edge of cardstock. Cut small piece of patterned paper, ink and adhere vertically to left portion of card. Ink and use adhesive dimensional dots to adhere snowman image to right portion of card. Adhere tab to upper left portion of image, tucking under snowman. Adhere button to tab using glue dot. Knot tulle and adhere to button using glue dot.
6. Adhere punched snowflake to lower portion of rectangular image using glue dot. Adhere jewels to center of snowflake. Print or stamp greeting to inside of card.

There's No Place Like Home Card
(also shown on page 58)
- large circular sticker or stamped image; small rectangular text sticker or stamp
- 4 colors of cardstock
- 3 coordinated patterned papers
- wide ribbon

Pink Patterned Purse Card
(continued from page 59)
1. Enlarge and trace purse pattern (page 155) onto paper and cut out. Trace scalloped topper onto cardstock and cut out. Fold scalloped piece in half to create purse shape (fold will be at the top).
2. Fold topper in half and adhere to folded edge of purse. Use punch to make two small holes in the fold for handle. Beginning inside the purse, run cord through both holes and knot to create handle.
3. Tie short lengths of ribbon to left side of handle. Punch small circles from coordinating cardstock and glue to each scallop on the topper. Thread floss through button and adhere with glue dot. Adhere gift card or money to the inside of card.

Holly Purse Card
(also shown on page 59)
- purse and topper patterns
- dotted cardstock plus 3 coordinating colors
- embossing template
- pearl string for handle
- border punch
- holly punch or die
- small hole punch or paper piercer
- adhesive, including fine-tipped glue
- computer or stamps for inside greeting
- adhesive hook and loop dot

1. Enlarge and trace purse and topper patterns (page 155) onto cardstock and cut out. Fold in half to create purse shape (fold will be at the bottom of purse). Fold topper and emboss the front. Adhere the INSIDE of it to the back side of the purse to create a flap/closure. Attach adhesive dot to the inside of the flap/closure and outside front of the purse. Use punch or piercer to

make two small holes in the fold for handle.
2. Cut out holly and berries and adhere to flap/closure. Punch border strip and mat with cardstock; adhere across bottom of purse. Adhere gift card or money to the inside of card.

Tinsel Purse Card
(also shown on page 59)
- rounded purse and topper patterns
- two colors cardstock
- embossing template
- wired tinsel
- small jingle bell
- floss
- narrow ribbon
- small punched or sticker snowflakes
- small hole punch
- adhesive, including liquid and fine-tipped glue
- computer or stamps for inside greeting
- hook and loop adhesive dot

1. Enlarge and trace purse and topper patterns (page 155) onto cardstock and cut out. Fold in half to create purse shape (fold will be at the bottom of purse). Emboss the FRONT of the purse. Fold topper and adhere the INSIDE of it to the back side of the purse to create a flap/closure.
2. Attach adhesive dot to the inside of the flap/closure and outside front of the purse. Use punch to make two small holes in the fold for handle. Beginning inside the purse, run ribbon through both holes and knot to create handle. Tie short lengths of ribbon to left side of handle. Cut a length of wired tinsel to fit along the flap; bend to form. Thread jingle bell with floss and tie snugly to the center of the cut piece of wire.
3. Use liquid glue to adhere the tinsel along the edge of the flap. Hold or weight in place to dry. Adhere small snowflakes to lower right portion of purse. Adhere gift card or money to the inside of card.

3-D Christmas Tree Gift Tag
(also shown on page 59)
- 3 colors of cardstock
- one patterned paper
- border punch
- punched star
- round sticker
- round stamp or computer for text
- circle punch slightly larger than round sticker and stamp
- floss
- wide ribbon
- adhesive, including strong tape and adhesive dimensional dots
- scoring blade
- corner rounder
- small hole punch

1. Cut a rectangle from cardstock to create tag. Round corners and punch hole at top. Cut patterned paper and adhere across center of tag. Punch a border from cardstock and adhere to lower portion of tag below patterned paper. Cut a narrow strip of contrasting cardstock and adhere just above border strip.
2. To make tree, cut 4 same-size narrow triangles from embossed cardstock. Score and fold each in half vertically. Adhere one side of the triangle to the facing side of another triangle until all 4 are adhered together. Adhere the flat side of this piece to the tag so that the tree "fans" out from the tag.
3. Cut and adhere a small cardstock trunk. Adhere punched star above tree. Create "to/from" using stamps or computer. Punch out using circle punch. Punch a cardstock circle of the same size to mat sticker. Adhere both pieces to the right portion of tag using pop dots. Tie ribbon through hole at top of tag.

Snowflake Tag
(also shown on page 59)
- large tag cut from cardstock
- 2 additional colors of cardstock
- 2-3 coordinating patterned papers
- die cut snowflake
- wide ribbon
- twine
- large and small button
- adhesive, including glue dots
- border punch
- computer or stamp for text

1. Cut a strip of patterned paper and adhere across upper portion of tag. Cut two narrow strips of patterned paper and adhere below the first strip. Punch a scalloped border from cardstock then back with a lighter color. Adhere along lower edge of tag. Print text on strip of light cardstock. Adhere across lower portion of card.
2. Adhere snowflake to tag. Adhere large button to snowflake center using glue dots. Thread twine through small button, tie in bow, then adhere small button to large button using glue dots. Double the wide ribbon and thread through tag hole. Tie and trim ends.

"Joy" Decoration
(also shown on page 61)
- large chipboard letters
- fine mist sparkle ink or acrylic paint
- patterned paper (preferably heavy double-sided paper)
- tracing paper
- ribbon
- twine
- snowflake punches or dies in two sizes
- glitter glue
- scissors
- sanding tool, such as a nail file
- white crafts glue
- adhesive dimensional dots
- brayer

1. Paint the edges of the chipboard using sparkle ink or acrylic paint. Allow to dry. Trace the letters onto patterned paper and cut out. Apply a thin coating of white glue to the front side of the chipboard letters and adhere the cut-out letter. Smooth with a brayer or the edge of a credit card and allow to dry. When letters are dry, sand the edges to reveal white core. Trace patterns (page 147) and cut out 2 sets of holly leaves and berries and lightly sand the edges. Punch or die cut 3 snowflakes; lightly cover with glitter glue. Allow to dry.
2. Adhere holly and berries to the letters "J" and "Y", using adhesive dimensional dots under berries. Tie ribbon around the top of the letter "J". Tie twine around the letter "Y". Adhere snowflakes to letter "O", placing one behind the letter.

Happy Snowman Wreath
(also shown on page 63)
1. Enlarge and trace patterns (page 156) onto tracing paper and cut out. Lay pattern for ball wrappings onto cotton batting and cut out. Wrap balls in cotton batting and pull edges together to completely cover plastic foam balls. Glue edges in place. Wrap white cotton yarn around balls, crossing yarns until ball is mostly covered. Some fleece pieces will show through.
2. Cut embellishments from scraps of felt, felted wool or fleece. **For Nordic hat,** cut one of pattern from felted wool. Place onto smaller ball and gather together top point about 1" from the end. Wrap length of embroidery floss tightly around end and knot at the back. Clip small pieces from the end of the point toward the wrapped string to make fringe. Chain stitch a length of thread from the ear points of the hat about 1$\frac{1}{2}$" down. Loop contrasting floss through the ends of the chained length and cut to make hat fringe.
3. **For ear muffs,** cut two circles from pattern. Roll cotton balls to make balls about 1" in size. Wrap fabric circles around balls and gather together at the back by stitching running stitches along the outside edges and pulling up thread tightly. Cut a thin strip of felted wool about 4$\frac{1}{2}$" long for the center of the ear muffs. Lay the strip over the ball at the top and pin in place, pushing straight pins through foam ball. Position muff circles over center band and tack in place by taking a couple hand stitches using matching sewing thread.
4. **For pointy stocking cap,** cut one of hat pattern from fabric desired. With right sides together, sew long slanted side seam using $\frac{1}{4}$" seam. Turn right side out. Slip over top of larger ball and fold up bottom for a little

cuff. At end point, sew loops of embroidery thread and clip to make tassel.
5. **For hoodie,** cut one piece 3$\frac{1}{2}$" x 9" from desired fabric. Fold long edge under $\frac{1}{2}$" to inside. Fold in half with short ends together and sew $\frac{1}{4}$" seam. Turn right side out and place over smaller ball. Cut a narrow strip of fabric about 9" long to tie into a bow. Stitch bow to bottom of hood with a few hand stitches.
6. Make scarves out of 1" wide strips of fabric, cutting ends in narrow pieces to make fringe. Loop around balls and knot in place. **For head band,** use 1" strip of felted wool and wrap around ball, tacking in place with a couple of hand stitches.
7. Make noses by cutting triangle-shaped patterns from orange felt. Fold in half and hand stitch close to edge to make a tube. Glue noses to balls. Glue beads to make eyes and mouth on each ball. If using as ornaments, sew a length of embroidery floss to the top as a hanger and knot in place.

Snowflakes Under Glass
(also shown on page 64)
- lightweight paper in desired color
- sharp scissors
- pencil
- charger, or underneath plate, in desired color
- one clear glass plate smaller than the charger plate

1. Use the patterns (page 153) or make your own snowflake patterns to measure the size desired for the plates you are using. Fold the paper as shown, below, and with a pencil mark the areas to be cut out.

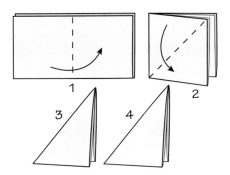

2. Use scissors to cut out the shapes. Unfold snowflake and press if desired using a cool iron. Place snowflake between plates.

No-Sew Fabric Trims

(continued from page 65)

1. Trace pattern (page 156) onto tracing paper and cut out. Cut shapes desired from cotton fabric, being generous in cutting shapes to cover the area desired. Lay first piece of fabric over plastic foam ball. Press paring knife blade at outside cut edge to work raw edges into ball.

2. Place adjoining fabric slightly over the pressed edge of previous fabric piece and press knife edge over raw edge to work it into the ball. Cut a length of trim and fold it in half to make loop. Poke cut ends of loop into ball at top and glue in place. Glue lengths of trim over edges of fabric.

Twine-Tied Candles

(also shown on page 65)
- purchased candles in desired sizes
- twine in variegated colors
- paper embellishments, button or charms
- short straight pins

1. Starting at the back of the candle, pin the twine to the candle. Begin wrapping the candle until desired width.

2. Thread a button or other embellishment on another piece of twine and wrap and pin in place. Tie a bow and pin to the front of candle if desired.

Never leave a burning candle unattended.

Peggy's Granola Tent Card Instructions

(also shown on page 68)
- patterned paper and 4 colors coordinating cardstock
- ribbon
- twine
- circle punches in 2 sizes to fit text, plus small hole punch
- tree punches or dies
- border punch or template
- scoring blade or board
- glitter glue
- stamps, rub-on letters or computer/ printer
- adhesive dimensional dots

1. Cut a 3" x 8" strip of cardstock for tag tent. Score at 1" from either end, then score at center of strip on the 4" mark. See diagram, below. Fold to create tent. Cut patterned paper to fit the front of tag. Punch a hole in the top of the tag. Punch cardstock border slightly wider than the tag and adhere to lower portion of tag.

2. Print or stamp label onto small circle, leaving room between words for twine. Wrap

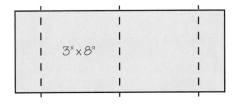

twine around circle; tie at side. Mat onto a larger circle of contrasting cardstock using pop dots and adhere to tag. Cut or punch trees from green cardstock, embellish with glitter glue and adhere to tag. Tie tag to container with pretty ribbon.

133

- crafts knife and straightedge ruler
- sanding tool
- candy canes
- hot-glue gun and hot glue sticks

For tag:
- embossed white cardstock
- candy cane die cut or pattern
- green dot/solid paper
- white/red dot paper
- circle punches in 2 sizes to fit text
- border punch
- black pen
- strong tape and adhesive dimensional dots
- stamps, rub-on letters or computer/printer

Fortune Cookie Box
(also shown on page 69)
- large size paper to fit pattern
- seasonal stamps
- scoring blade or scoring board
- narrow ribbon for box handle
- piercing tool
- contrasting cardstock and matching patterned paper
- small scalloped dies or punches
- small circle punches
- stamps, rub-on letters or computer/printer

1. Enlarge and trace the box pattern (page 157) onto large size paper. Cut out and score as indicated. Make holes using piercing tools as specified on pattern. Fold into box shape. Unfold and stamp box using seasonal stamp. Allow to dry then refold box. Thread ribbon through holes and secure with knots on the inside of the box.
2. Decorate sides of box with scalloped shapes cut from contrasting shades of cardstock. Add circles to center of shapes.
3. For tag, cut rectangle from patterned paper. Notch the corners using a circle punch. Cut a slightly larger mat from contrasting cardstock and notch corners. Adhere the pieces together. Cut a strip of coordinating patterned paper and adhere across the center of the tag. Cut scalloped shape for the center of the tag and print/stamp with "For You". Adhere to tag base using adhesive dimensional dots. Adhere or tie tag to box as desired.

Apple-Ginger Chutney Jar Topper
(also shown on page 70)
- 4 colors coordinating papers or cardstock
- circle cutter or template
- stamps, rub-on letters or computer/printer
- ribbon
- chipboard
- strong tape adhesive

1. Cut a circle of chipboard (or 2-3 pieces of cardstock) and adhere to the indented portion of the lid to create a flat surface. Cut 4 circles of coordinating papers to fit the jar lid insert. (Our jar lid measures 3".)
2. Fold each circle in fourths and cut apart. Add text to two of the pieces. Adhere all four pieces to the lid. Wrap ribbon around the lid ring and tie at side. (Tip: If ribbon is too wide for the ring, fold in half and iron to secure. Run a narrow strip of tape adhesive around the jar ring to hold ribbon in place.)

See-Through Brownie Box
(also shown on page 72)
For box:
- large box for brownies
- wide ribbon to fit edges of box lid
- white and red cardstock
- cellophane

1. To make box, cover box base with white cardstock. Cut strips of red cardstock and adhere vertically to the sides of the box. For lid, determine size of opening and make pattern from scratch paper. Adhere to box lid where desired. Use crafts knife and straightedge to carefully cut opening in lid. Use sanding tool to smooth rough edges. Cut a piece of cellophane to fit over the opening, then adhere to box lid. Cut white cardstock to fit top of lid, then cut a hole in the cardstock to match the hole in the lid. Adhere to box lid. Cut narrow strips of red cardstock to fit around the opening, covering any exposed edges. Cut a similar sized piece of white cardstock to line the inside of the lid. Trim with narrow strips of white cardstock. Adhere wide ribbon around the edges of the box lid using strong tape adhesive. Adhere candy canes to lid using hot glue.
2. For tag, trace pattern (page 153). Trace onto embossed white cardstock and cut out; punch hole in top. Adhere green paper across the center of the tag, then add a strip of white/red dot paper below it.
3. Adhere border punched from red cardstock to lower portion of tag. Create cane from white and red cardstock, then add green bow. Add details using black pen and adhere using dimensional dots. Print "For You" and punch into small circle. Add dots around circle with black pen. Mat with a larger circle punched from red cardstock. Adhere to tag using adhesive dimensional dots. Attach tag to box with same ribbon used on box.

Candy Sleigh Holder

(also shown on page 73)

- tracing paper
- pencil
- 12" square of heavy scrapbook paper
- scissors
- low-temp glue gun and glue sticks
- chenille stems
- candy canes

1. Enlarge and trace the sleigh pattern (page 150) and cut out, paying close attention to cutting and folding marks. Use pattern to cut a sleigh from scrapbook paper.
2. Fold on indicated lines and glue together. Glue chenille stem around the top edges, piecing to fit. Glue a pair of candy cane runners on the bottom of each sleigh.

Paper Poppers

(also shown on page 73)

- short cardboard tubes
- scissors
- 2 coordinating scrapbook papers
- decorative-edge scissors
- tape
- metallic chenille stems
- cupcake liners
- hot-glue gun and glue sticks

1. Using one of the scrapbook papers, cut a piece to fit around the cardboard tube allowing ends to overlap slightly. Wrap the tube with the paper piece, securing with tape at the end. Using decorative-edge scissors, cut a strip from the coordinating paper, 2 inches narrower than the tube, and tape it centered around the tube.
2. Hot-glue pieces of chenille stem around each tube end, shaping them to fit the curve. Hot-glue a cupcake liner in one tube end. Fill the popper with wrapped candies or other small surprises. Hot-glue a second cupcake liner in the remaining tube end.

Country Herb Spread Gift Box

(also shown on page 74)

- box for crackers
- glass container for dip
- patterned paper and coordinating cardstock
- self-adhesive jewels
- corner rounder
- ink
- stamps, rub-on letters or computer/ printer

1. Cut patterned paper to fit sides and tops of containers. Round corners, ink and adhere to containers.
2. Print "Crispy Wheat Crackers" on paper leaving space for jewels. Cut strip to fit box lid and adhere. Add self-adhesive jewels.

Decorated Pretzel Jar

(also shown on page 75)

- clear jar with hinge top
- 2-3 coordinated patterned papers and cardstock
- circle cutter or template
- star punch or die
- self-adhesive silver jewels or gems
- adhesive, including strong tape
- ribbon or raffia
- stamps, rub-on letters or computer/ printer
- brown ink pen

1. For jar, cut a circle from cardstock to fit the lid and adhere. Embellish lid with stars punched or cut from coordinating cardstock. Cut patterned paper strip to fit around the jar. Mat with a slightly wider strip of cardstock and adhere firmly to the jar using tape adhesive. Print or stamp label on white cardstock and mat. Adhere stars to the bottom of the label. Add jewels to the center of each star. Adhere completed label to front of the jar using strong adhesive.
2. For pretzel, cut out pretzel pattern (page 152) from tan cardstock. Write "For You" with matching pen on inside of pretzel tag. Tie to the jar using raffia.

Candy Tin

(also shown on page 75)
- plain round tin
- 2 or more coordinating scrapbook papers
- decorative-edge scissors
- drill, awl or ice pick
- hot-glue gun and glue sticks
- wire
- large decorative jingle bell
- ribbon
- pine cone and greenery picks

1. To create a decorative background for the tin topper, trace around bowls or other round objects that are smaller than the tin lid. Cut out 2 or more circles from scrapbook paper. Drill or poke 2 holes near the center of the lid.

2. Layer the paper circles, the smaller circle centered on the larger one. Center them on the lid and mark where the lid punctures are located. Poke holes through both layers of paper. Aligning holes, hot-glue the papers together and to the lid. Wire jingle bell to lid through holes. Tie on a ribbon bow and hot-glue pine cone and greenery picks extending from bell.

S'mores Container and Decorated Tag

(also shown on page 76)
- small brown paper sacks
- small piece of cardboard to fit into sack
- crafts knife
- small cellophane sacks
- ceramic bread pan
- white and brown cardstock
- twine
- brown ink
- small hole punch
- piercing tool
- small stick
- hot-glue gun and glue sticks
- stamps, rub-on letters or computer/printer

1. To make the sacks, enlarge and trace patterns (page 146). Trace around shape onto front of paper sack. Slide a heavy piece of cardboard into sack and cut out with crafts knife. Slide cellophane bag into sack to hold food.

2. To make the tag, print "S'mores" on white cardstock and trim to rectangular shape. Punch a small hole in the upper corners of the cardstock. Print "Campfire Treats" and "For You" in small letters on kraft cardstock, then cut into tag shapes and ink. Use piercing tool to make holes in the top of the two small tags. Cut a small stick slightly wider than the white tag. Thread twine through the holes on the small tags, then tie the tags to the stick. Adhere stick to the white tag using hot glue. Thread twine through the holes at top of tag, then tie or secure the tag to the side of the bread pan.

Spicy Fruit Tea Mix

(also shown on page 76)
- clear glass jar with lid
- china or ceramic cup
- crafts glue
- 1" w ribbon
- small piece of felt
- embroidery floss and needle
- scrap of solid color cardstock
- scrap of white paper

1. Be sure the jar is clean and dry. Glue the ribbon around jar top. Glue the cup to the jar top. Set aside.

2. Using the pattern (page 152) cut out the felt label. Work embroidery stitches on the felt label front referring to pattern. Cut another piece of felt and lay on back of embroidered piece. Stitch around sides and bottom leaving an opening at the top. Sew or glue a piece of ribbon to the back of the felt tag. Wrap around the jar and secure in the back with a stitch or glue.

3. Make the instructions tag by printing the instructions on the white paper. Glue to the colored cardstock. Slide inside felt opening.

General Instructions

Making Patterns

When the entire pattern is shown, place tracing or tissue paper over the pattern and draw over the lines. For a more durable pattern, use a permanent marker to draw over the pattern on stencil plastic—this is sometimes also called a template.

When only half of the pattern is shown (indicated by a dotted line on the pattern), fold the tracing paper in half. Place the fold along the dotted line and trace the pattern half. Turn the folded paper over and draw over the traced lines on the remaining side. Unfold the pattern and cut it out.

Sizing Patterns

To change the size of the pattern, divide the desired height or width of the pattern (whichever is greater) by the actual height or width of the pattern. Multiply the result by 100 and photocopy the pattern at this percentage.

For example: You want your pattern to be 8"h, but the pattern on the page is 6"h. So 8:6=1.33x100=133%. Copy the pattern at 133%.

If your copier doesn't enlarge to the size you need, enlarge the pattern to the maximum percentage on the copier. Then repeat step 1, dividing the desired size by the size of the enlarged pattern. Multiply this result by 100 and photocopy the enlarged pattern at the new percentage.

For very large projects, you'll need to enlarge the design in sections onto separate sheets of paper. Repeat as needed to reach the desired size and tape the pattern pieces together.

Transferring Patterns to Fabrics

Trace the pattern onto tissue paper. Pin the tissue paper to the felt or fabric and stitch through the paper. Carefully tear the tissue paper away.

Transferring Patterns To Cardstock Or Other Materials

Trace the pattern onto tracing paper. Place the pattern on the cardstock (or whatever material you are transferring to) and use a pencil to lightly draw around the pattern. For pattern details, slip transfer paper between the pattern and the cardstock and draw over the detail lines.

Cutting a Stencil

Enlarge the pattern if necessary. Using a fine-point permanent marker, trace the pattern onto stencil plastic or mylar. Carefully cut the plastic with scissors or a crafts knife, making sure all edges are smooth.

Making a Fabric Circle

Matching right sides, fold the fabric square in half from top to bottom and again from left to right. Tie one end of a length of string to a water-soluble marking pen; insert a thumbtack through the string at the length indicated in the project instructions. Insert the thumbtack through the folded corner of the fabric. Holding the tack in place and keeping the string taut, mark the cutting line (Fig. 1).

Fig. 1

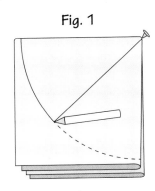

Embroidery Stitches

Always come up at 1 and all odd numbers and go down at 2 and all even numbers unless otherwise indicated.

Backstitch

Bring the needle up at 1, go down at 2, come up at 3 and go down at 4 (Fig. 2).

Fig. 2

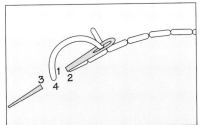

Blanket Stitch

Referring to Fig. 3, bring the needle up at 1. Keeping the thread below the point of the needle, go down at 2 and come up at 3. Continue working as shown in Fig. 4.

Fig. 3

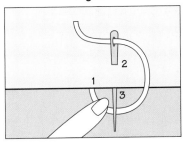

Fig. 4

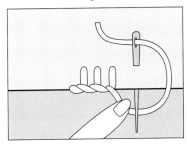

Bullion Knot

Referring to Fig. 5, bring the needle up at 1 and take the needle down at 2 (this is the distance the knot will cover); come up at 1 again and wrap the yarn around the needle as many times as necessary to cover the distance between 1 and 2. Pull needle through wraps and adjust on the 1-2 loop (Figs. 6-7).

Fig. 5

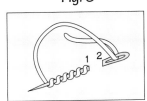

Fig. 6

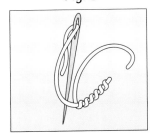

Anchor the knot with a small straight stitch at 2 (Fig. 8).

Fig. 7

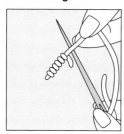

Fig. 8

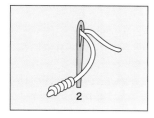

CHAIN STITCH

Referring to Fig. 9, bring the needle up at 1; take the needle down again at 1 to form a loop. Bring the needle up at 2; take the needle down again at 2 to form a second loop (Fig. 10). Continue making loops. Anchor the last chain with a small straight stitch (Fig. 11).

Fig. 9

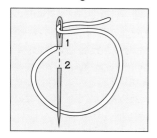

Fig. 10

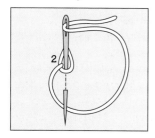

Fig. 11

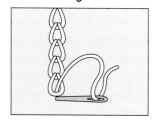

COUCHING STITCH

Referring to Fig. 12, lay the thread to be couched on the fabric; bring the needle up at 1 and go down at 2. Continue until entire thread length is couched.

Fig. 12

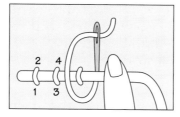

CROSS STITCH

Bring the needle up at 1 and go down at 2. Come up at 3 and go down at 4 (Fig.13).

Fig. 13

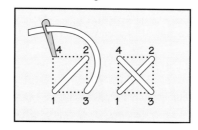

For the horizontal rows, work the stitches in 2 journeys (Fig. 14).

Fig. 14

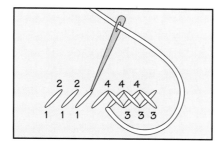

FERN STITCH

Referring to Fig. 15, work the central spine first then stitch a straight stitch either side of that spine. Bring needle up at 1, down at 2, up at 3, down at 4 and up at 5.

Fig. 15

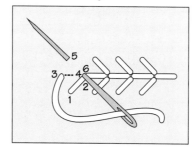

FLY STITCH

Refer to Fig. 16. Fly Stitch is also known as "Y" Stitch. It is worked making a V-shaped loop which is then tied down by a vertical Straight Stitch. Bring needle through the fabric out at the top and to the left of the line that is to be worked.

Fig. 16

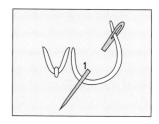

FRENCH KNOT

Referring to Fig. 17, bring the needle up at 1. Wrap the floss once around the needle and insert the needle at 2, holding the floss end with non-stitching fingers. Tighten the knot; then, pull the needle through the fabric, holding the floss until it must be released. For larger knot, use more strands; wrap only once.

Fig. 17

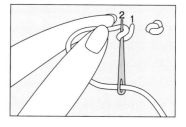

LAZY DAISY

Bring the needle up at 1; take the needle back down at 1 to form a loop and bring the needle up at 2. Keeping the loop below the point of the needle (Fig. 18), take the needle down at 3 to anchor the loop.

Fig. 18

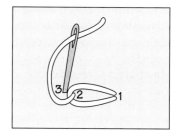

Running Stitch

Referring to Fig. 19, make a series of straight stitches with the stitch length equal to the space between stitches.

Fig. 19

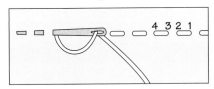

Stem Stitch

Referring to Fig. 20, come up at 1. Keeping the thread below the stitching line, go down at 2 and come up at 3. Go down at 4 and come up at 5.

Fig. 20

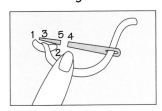

Straight Stitch

Referring to Fig. 21, come up at 1 and go down at 2.

Fig. 21

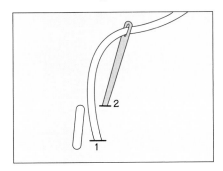

Needle Felting

Needle Felting uses wool roving. Wool roving can be purchased at fabric and crafts stores and online. It can be worked into shape by itself using a special needle felting needle and mat. Or, you can apply wool roving to a background fabric using a needle felting tool and mat. Lightly punch the needles to interlock the fibers and join the pieces without sewing or gluing. The brush-like mat allows the needles to easily pierce the fibers. We used the Clover® Felting Needle Tool to make our projects—it has a locking plastic shield that provides protection from the sharp needles.

Pom-poms

For a 2" diameter pom-pom, place an 8" piece of yarn along one long edge of a 1"x3" cardboard strip. Wrap yarn around and around the strip and yarn piece (Fig. 22). (The more you wrap, the fluffier the pom-pom.) Tie the wound yarn together tightly with the 8" piece. Leaving the tie ends long to attach the pom-pom, cut the loops opposite the tie; then, fluff and trim the pom-pom into a smooth ball.

Fig. 22

Making Yo-Yo's

To make each yo-yo, cut a circle as indicated in the project instructions. Press the circle edge ¼" to the wrong side. Referring to Fig. 23, sew Running Stitches around the edge with a doubled strand of thread. Referring to Fig. 24, pull the thread tightly to gather. Knot and trim the thread end. Flatten the yo-yo with the small opening at the center of the circle.

Fig. 23

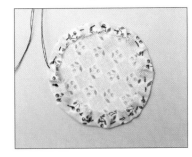

Fig. 24

Crochet Abbreviations

Abbreviations

ch(s)	chain(s)
cm	centimeters
dc	double crochet
hdc	half double crochet
lp(s)	loop(s)
mm	millimeters
sl st	slip stitch
sc(s)	single crochet(s)
st(s)	stitch(es)
tr	treble crochet

*—work instructions following * as many **more** times as indicated in addition to the first time. *
( ) or [ ] — contains explanatory remarks
colon (:) — the number given after a colon at the end of a row denotes the number of stitches you should have on that row.

Gauge

Exact gauge is essential for proper fit. Before beginning your project, make a sample swatch in the yarn and hook specified. After completing the swatch, measure it, counting your stitches and rows or rounds carefully. If your swatch is larger or smaller than specified, make another, changing hook size to get the correct gauge. Keep trying until you find the size hook that will give you the specified gauge.

Felting Sweaters

Felting sweaters brings the fibers in the sweater closer together to make it more compact. The texture becomes more interesting. Always use 100% wool sweaters when you wish to felt a sweater. Using sweaters with less than 90% wool will not work for felted sweater projects.

Place the sweater inside an old pillowcase and wash in very hot water in the washing machine. **Note:** Washing the sweater in the pillowcase keeps little fibers from getting into the machine works.

Use a little regular washing detergent when felting. Then rinse the sweaters in hot water and dry in a hot dryer. Press the wool before cutting out the pieces. Tightly felted wool does not ravel and can be left unfinished similar to using purchased wool felt.

Fabric Christmas Cookie Ornaments
(page 10)

Felted Holly Trim
(page 12)
Enlarge 200%

Gingerbread House Garland
(page 11)

Fold

Fold

Fruit-Inspired Luminarias
(page 13)

Fabric Christmas Cookie Ornaments
(page 10)

Roof Edge attaches here

House Side

Cut 2 in same color as gabled side and 1 in darker color for the base

Base Edge attaches here

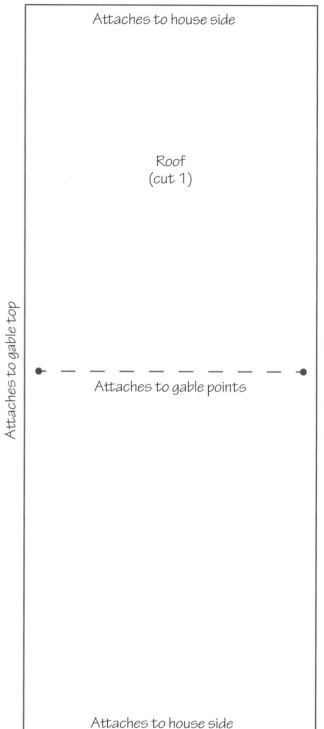

Attaches to house side

Roof
(cut 1)

Attaches to gable top

Attaches to gable points

Attaches to gable top

Attaches to house side

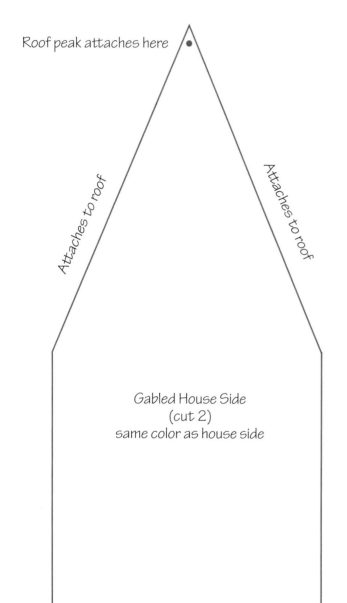

Roof peak attaches here

Attaches to roof

Attaches to roof

Gabled House Side
(cut 2)
same color as house side

Attaches to base

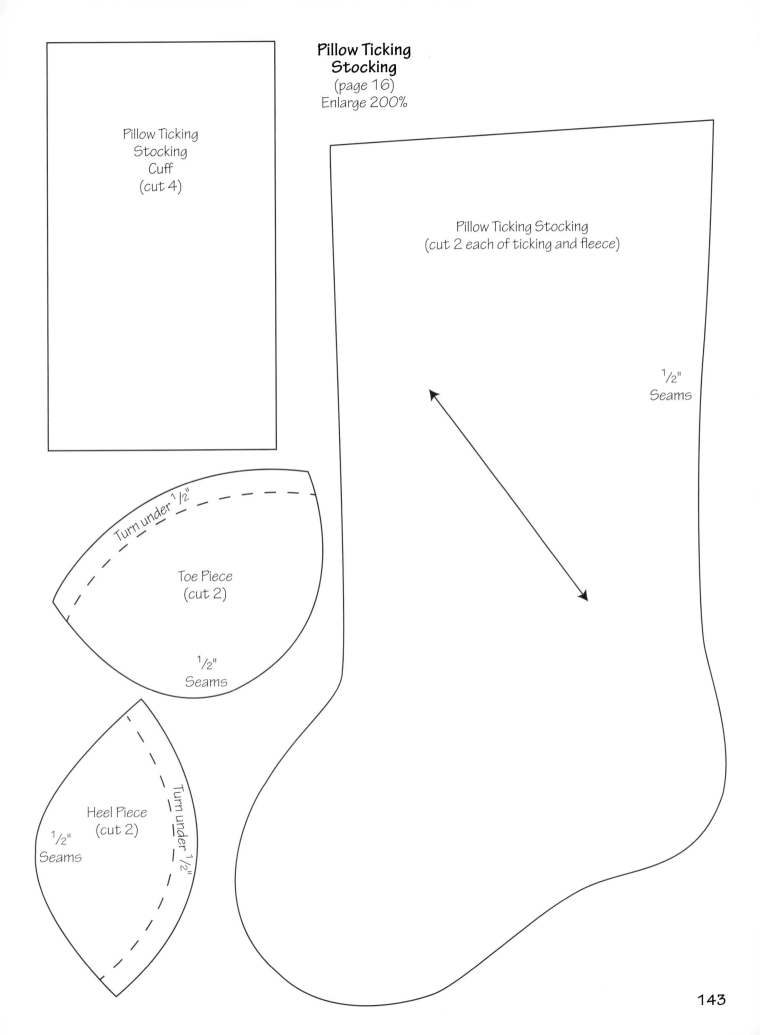

Pillow Ticking
Stocking
Cuff
(cut 4)

**Pillow Ticking
Stocking**
(page 16)
Enlarge 200%

Pillow Ticking Stocking
(cut 2 each of ticking and fleece)

$^1/_2$"
Seams

Turn under $^1/_2$"

Toe Piece
(cut 2)

$^1/_2$"
Seams

Heel Piece
(cut 2)

Turn under $^1/_2$"

$^1/_2$"
Seams

143

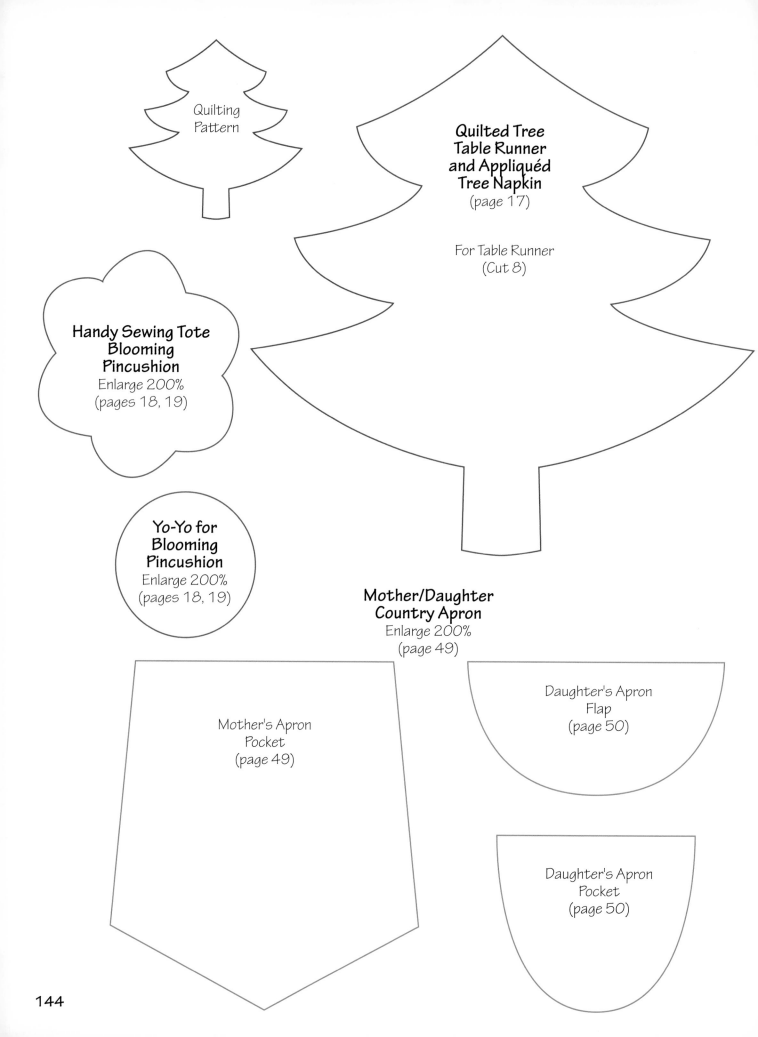

Quilting
Pattern

Quilted Tree
Table Runner
and Appliquéd
Tree Napkin
(page 17)

For Table Runner
(Cut 8)

Handy Sewing Tote
Blooming
Pincushion
Enlarge 200%
(pages 18, 19)

Yo-Yo for
Blooming
Pincushion
Enlarge 200%
(pages 18, 19)

Mother/Daughter
Country Apron
Enlarge 200%
(page 49)

Daughter's Apron
Flap
(page 50)

Mother's Apron
Pocket
(page 49)

Daughter's Apron
Pocket
(page 50)

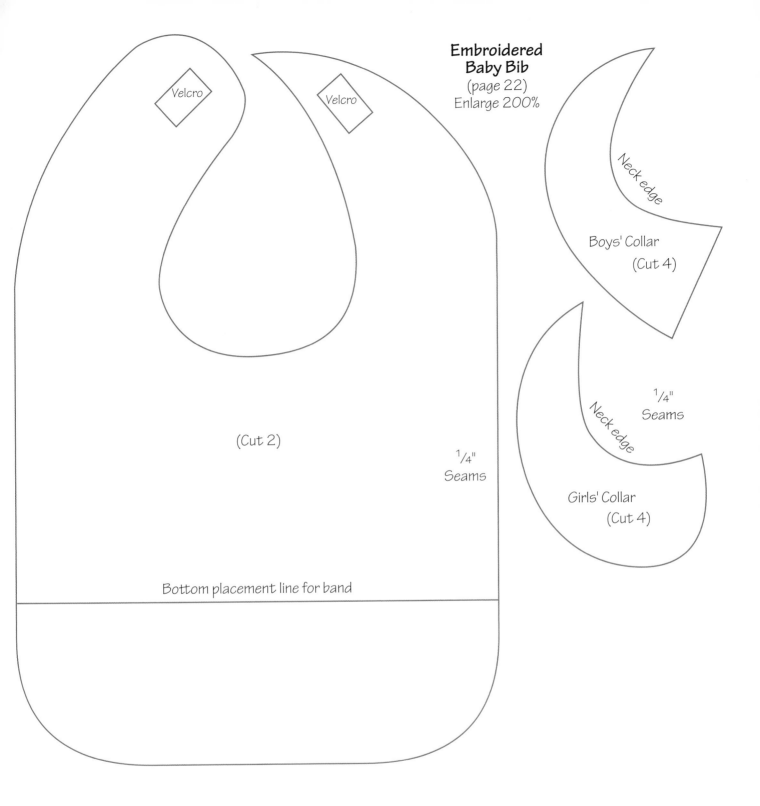

Velcro

Velcro

Embroidered Baby Bib
(page 22)
Enlarge 200%

Neck edge

Boys' Collar
(Cut 4)

Neck edge

¼"
Seams

Girls' Collar
(Cut 4)

(Cut 2)

¼"
Seams

Bottom placement line for band

Full Size Embroidery
Pattern for Baby Bibs

*Sweet Baby
Little Boy Blue*

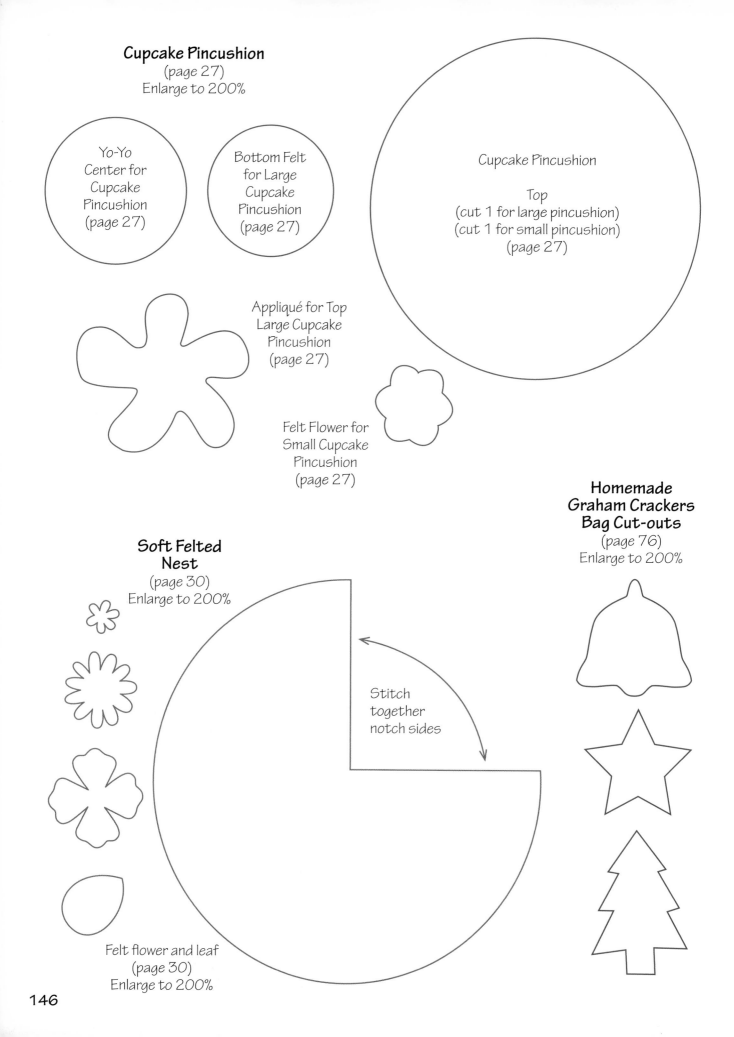

Cupcake Pincushion
(page 27)
Enlarge to 200%

Yo-Yo Center for Cupcake Pincushion (page 27)

Bottom Felt for Large Cupcake Pincushion (page 27)

Cupcake Pincushion

Top
(cut 1 for large pincushion)
(cut 1 for small pincushion)
(page 27)

Appliqué for Top Large Cupcake Pincushion (page 27)

Felt Flower for Small Cupcake Pincushion (page 27)

Homemade Graham Crackers Bag Cut-outs
(page 76)
Enlarge to 200%

Soft Felted Nest
(page 30)
Enlarge to 200%

Stitch together notch sides

Felt flower and leaf (page 30)
Enlarge to 200%

146

Wool Snowflakes
(page 32-33)
Enlarge 200%

Wool Snowflake
Background
shapes
Enlarge 200%

"Joy" Decoration
Holly and Berries
(page 61)

Lightly fold leaf in half
emboss with pattern

Sweet Sister
Dolls
(page 38)

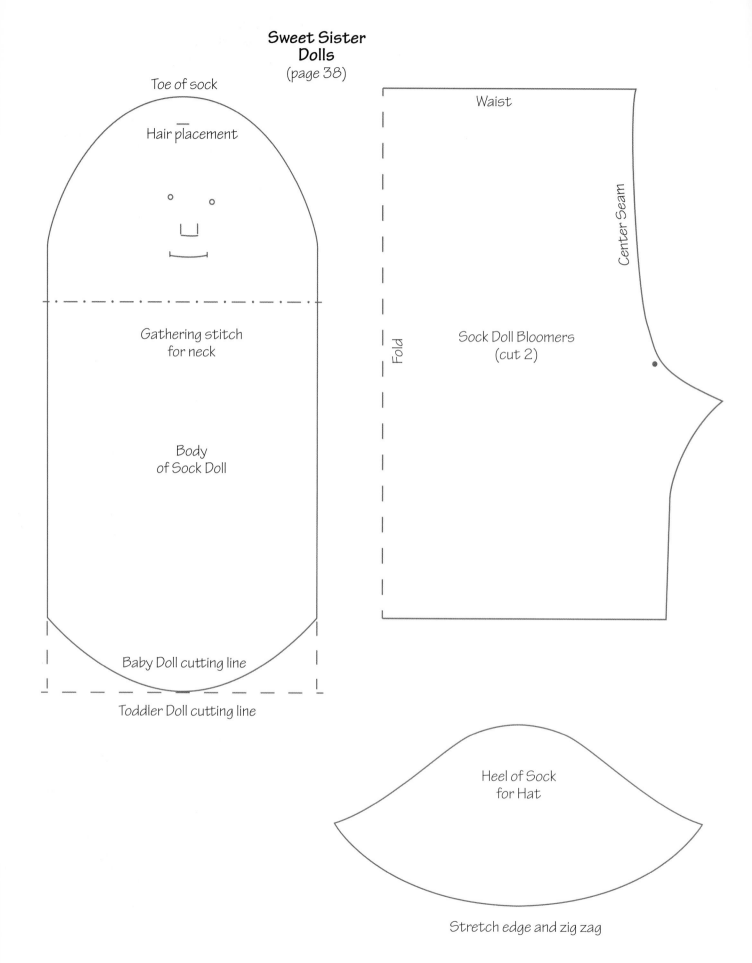

Toe of sock

Hair placement

Gathering stitch
for neck

Body
of Sock Doll

Baby Doll cutting line

Toddler Doll cutting line

Waist

Center Seam

Fold

Sock Doll Bloomers
(cut 2)

Heel of Sock
for Hat

Stretch edge and zig zag

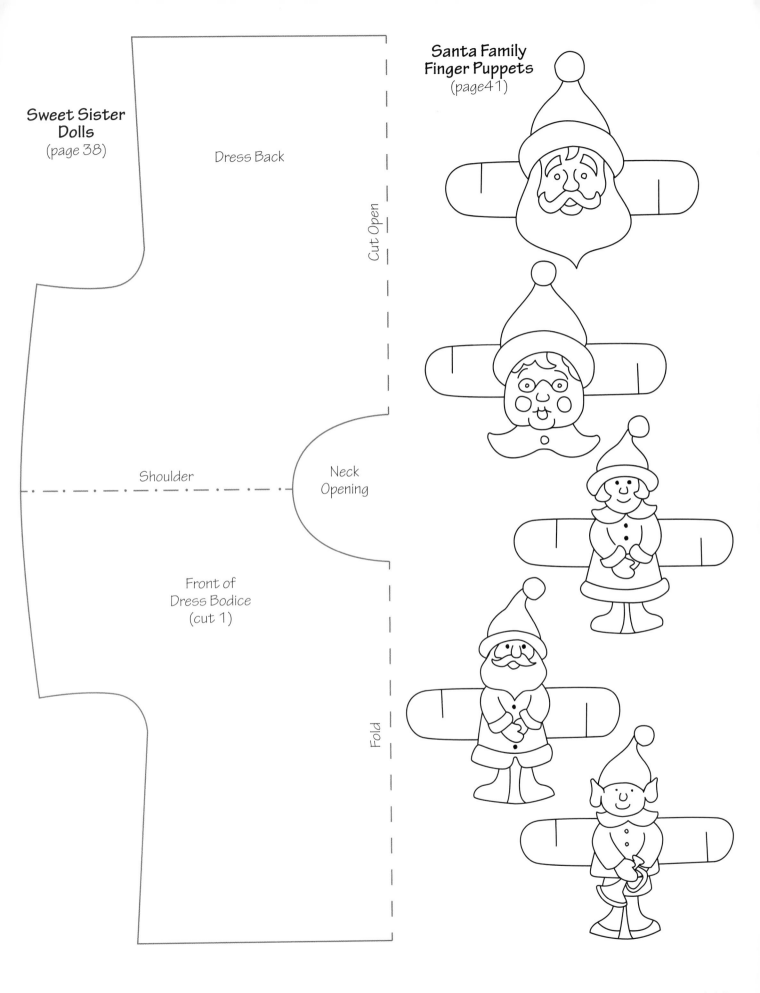

Sweet Sister Dolls
(page 38)

Dress Back

Cut Open

Shoulder

Neck Opening

Front of Dress Bodice (cut 1)

Fold

Santa Family Finger Puppets
(page41)

Paper Doll Dress Trims
(page 39)
Enlarge 200%

**Snowy Trail Mix
Candy Sleigh Holder**
(page 73)
Enlarge 200%

Fold

Fold

Fold

Fold

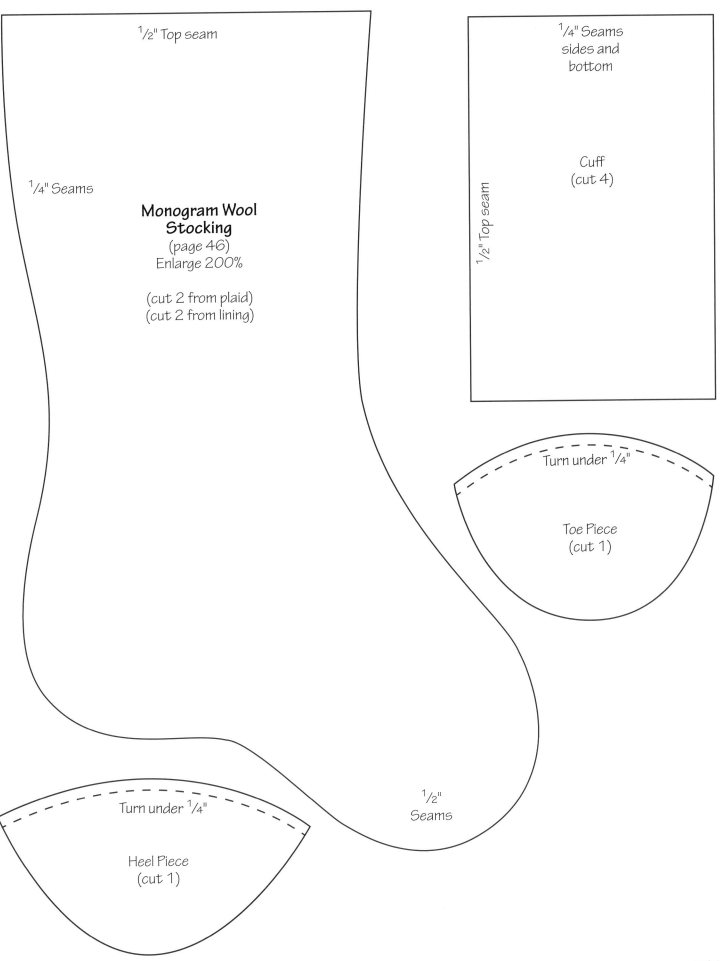

½" Top seam

¼" Seams

Monogram Wool Stocking
(page 46)
Enlarge 200%

(cut 2 from plaid)
(cut 2 from lining)

¼" Seams
sides and
bottom

Cuff
(cut 4)

½" Top seam

Turn under ¼"

Toe Piece
(cut 1)

½"
Seams

Turn under ¼"

Heel Piece
(cut 1)

½" Top seam

Cozy Mug Wraps
(page 47)
Enlarge 200%

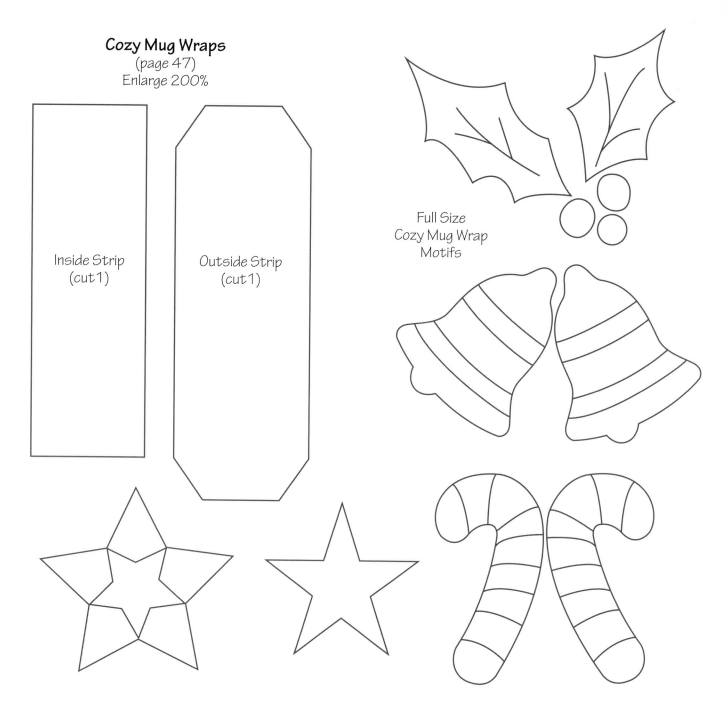

Inside Strip
(cut 1)

Outside Strip
(cut 1)

Full Size
Cozy Mug Wrap
Motifs

Spicy Fruit Tea Mix Tag
(page 76)

Spicy Fruit Tea Mix

Pretzels with Pizzazz Tag
(page 75)

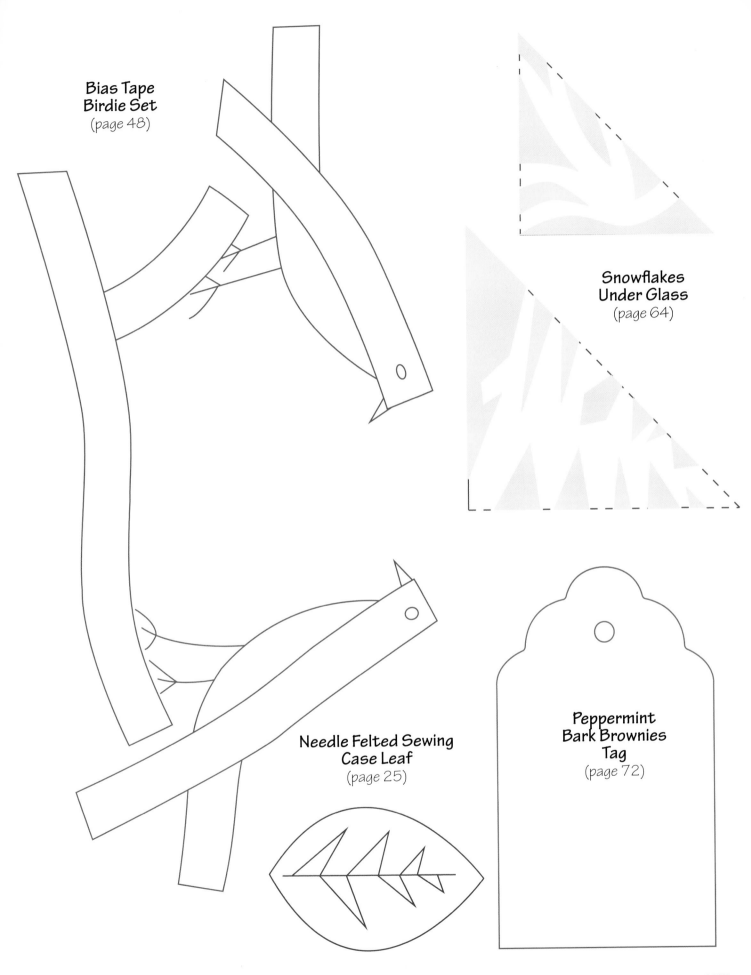

Bias Tape
Birdie Set
(page 48)

Snowflakes
Under Glass
(page 64)

Needle Felted Sewing
Case Leaf
(page 25)

Peppermint
Bark Brownies
Tag
(page 72)

153

Poinsettia Topper
(page 55)

Leaf

Flower
(cut 2)

Dressed-Up Doggy Cards
(page 56)

Ear

Poodle Body

Poodle collar
(cut 1)

Poodle Coat
(cut 1)

Ear

Dachshund body

Dachshund Coat
(cut 1)

154

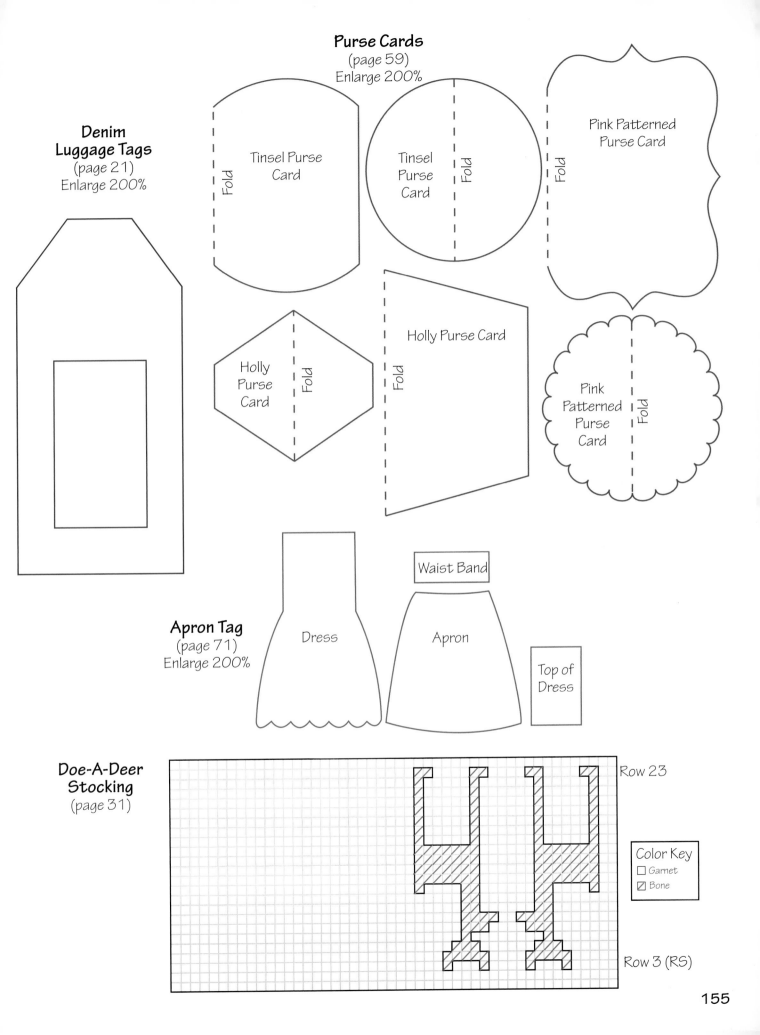

Denim Luggage Tags
(page 21)
Enlarge 200%

Purse Cards
(page 59)
Enlarge 200%

Tinsel Purse Card

Fold

Tinsel Purse Card

Fold

Pink Patterned Purse Card

Fold

Holly Purse Card

Fold

Holly Purse Card

Fold

Holly Purse Card

Fold

Pink Patterned Purse Card

Fold

Apron Tag
(page 71)
Enlarge 200%

Dress

Waist Band

Apron

Top of Dress

Doe-A-Deer Stocking
(page 31)

Row 23

Color Key
☐ Garnet
☒ Bone

Row 3 (RS)

155

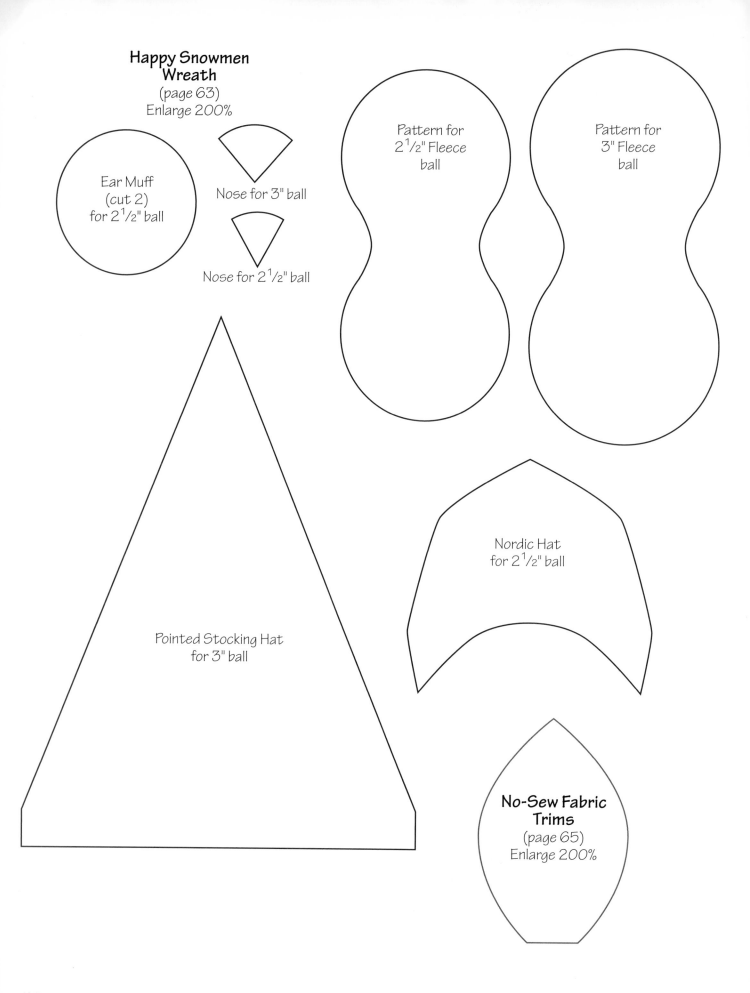

Happy Snowmen Wreath
(page 63)
Enlarge 200%

Ear Muff
(cut 2)
for 2$\frac{1}{2}$" ball

Nose for 3" ball

Nose for 2$\frac{1}{2}$" ball

Pattern for 2$\frac{1}{2}$" Fleece ball

Pattern for 3" Fleece ball

Pointed Stocking Hat for 3" ball

Nordic Hat for 2$\frac{1}{2}$" ball

No-Sew Fabric Trims
(page 65)
Enlarge 200%

Jumbo Fortune Cookie Box
(page 69)
Enlarge 200%

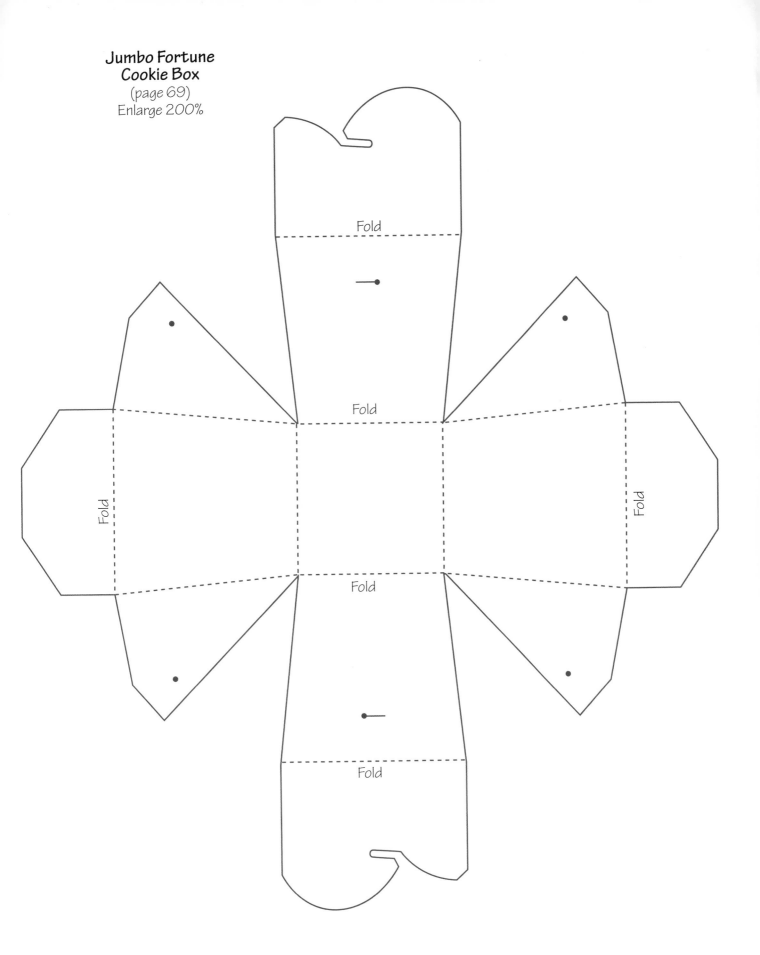

Fold

Fold

Fold

Fold

Fold

Fold

Project Index

Recipe Index

IT'S HARD TO BE GOOD.

Credits

We want to extend a warm "thank you!" to so many people who helped to create this book:

We want to thank Jay Wilde Photography, Primary Image/Dean Tanner, Becky Luigart-Stayner, Mindi Shapiro Levine and Ana Price Kelly for their excellent work.

It takes quality supplies to make beautiful projects. These are some of the companies that we used to make the crafts and decorating projects in the book: DMC Corporation for embroidery floss, Clover Needlecraft, Inc., for needle felting supplies, Bazzill Basics for many of the paper crafts, National Nonwovens for superior felting supplies, Bobs Candies for candy sticks and canes and Caron Simply Soft® for yarns.

Thank you to Martin Schmidt & Sons in Portland, Oregon for the beautiful Christmas trees, fresh greenery and wreaths we used in the photos.

A special thank you to Eunella Neymeyer for the use of her antique miniature sewing machine and vintage children's books and to Ardith Field for the use of her vintage kitchen collection and antique linens.

We want to thank our special models: Currin, Elizabeth, Grace and Priya for sharing their modeling talents with us.

A very special thank you to Julie and Rob Anliker and LuAnn and Jim Brandsen, who allowed us to photograph some of the projects in their beautiful homes.

If these cozy Christmas ideas have inspired you to look for more Gooseberry Patch® publications, find us online at www.gooseberrypatch.com and see what's new. We're on Facebook and Twitter too, so you can keep up with us even more often!